# AS WE WERE

First published in 2004 by

WOODFIELD PUBLISHING
Bognor Regis, West Sussex, England
www.woodfieldpublishing.com

ISBN 1-903953-76-6

# As We Were

*The lives, loves and memories of those who
served in the Women's Auxiliary Air Force*

EDITED BY
**BERYL R WILLIAMS**

Woodfield

Young WAAF volunteers from Plymouth in 1939. Front row, left is Margaret Swann née Brennan, who became a Flight Sergeant in Accounts.

Victory Parade 1945

*This book is dedicated to past members of the WAAF, including all members of the WAAF Association.*

*All royalties earned will be donated to RAF Charities.*

Babs Sargent, Musician    Sgt Mary Blue, Messing NCO

Ruby Mallinson, Clerk GD    Sgt Pat Fisher, Admin

# Contents

vi

# Foreword

Beryl Williams, in her compilation of personal reminiscences by former members of the Women's Auxiliary Air Force, takes us back to wartime Britain and vividly captures that spirit of comradeship, the hallmark of the armed services, which sustained the morale of the nation during its darkest days.

As one of the individuals who joined the RAF straight from boarding school as a 'Trenchard Brat' (aircraft apprentice) in 1936 at the age of 15 years, served for 40 years, married a member of the WAAF in 1941 (still going strong!) and is still associated with the RAF, I might be seen as a 'dyed-in-the wool old sweat' with limited interests.

True or not, the readers of this absorbing book need not share a similar background to be assured of huge enjoyment of its contents.

**Group Captain the Earl of Ilchester**

# *About the Editor*

Beryl Williams (née Stockwell) was a published writer of fiction and non-fiction. Her short stories were published in national magazines, newspapers and collections. She published a book about the WAAF marching bands and a short memoir of Elva Blacker, a painter who served as a WAAF at Biggin Hill (see 'An Artist in the WAAF' on page 120).

Beryl in 1943

Enlisting in the WAAF in early 1941, Beryl served for four and a half years. Marrying a regular serviceman, the following years were spent with her husband on his postings, together with their three children, living in married quarters in Britain and overseas.

Beryl edited *WAAFA News*, the journal of the WAAF Association for ten years until May 2003.

Sadly, Beryl died in March 2004, before the publication of this book, into which she had put so much time and effort.

# Acknowledgements

In the writing and compilation of this book, my thanks are due to many others. To all the ladies who allowed the use of their stories and photographs. To all who gave permission to use other photographs, especially the RAF Museum and the Imperial War Museum for their ready agreement to my reprinting of photographs from their archives.

My sincere thanks to the Earl of Ilchester for writing the Foreword.

To Rod Priddle, for permission to print the poem *Dusk Take-Off, 1940* by Ronald Ransom from his book *A Wing and a Prayer* (Wilbek & Lewbar)

To Victor Selwyn MBE Editor, for permission to print the poem *Missing* by Herbert Corby from *The Voice Of War* (Penguin Books 1996)

To my son Robert Williams, for his wise judgement and help in my work

And last but not least to my husband for his forbearance.

If I have left any person out, or not given an acknowledgement to their work I apologise. Every effort has been made to contact copyright holders.

B.W.

# References

## Books

K. Bentley Beauman, *Wings on her Shoulders* (Hutchinson 1945)

Sqn Ldr Beryl E. Escott, *Women in Air Force Blue* (Patrick Stephens Ltd 1989)

Sqn Ldr Beryl E. Escott, *Twentieth Century Women of Courage* (Sutton 1999)

Jenny Filby & Geoff Clark, *Not All Airmen Fly* (Epping Forest District Council 1994)

Beryl R. Williams, *They Shall Have Music* (Brigwill 1995)

Ian B. Wright, *The Silken Saviour* (Glen Graphics 2001)

## Magazines

Sqn Ldr Tony Freeman AE RAuxAF. 'A History of Women's Service with the RAF' in *Air Clues*, April 1998, pp 157-162

*WAAF Association News*, Issues 5-31

Stan White, Editor, *Salute to Women of the RAF* (RAFA Ads Ltd.)

# Preface

Today, career opportunities for women are taken for granted. Equal opportunities with men are offered in an ever-growing number of occupations. It was not always so. Women have had to fight hard for the right. During World War I, thousands of women joined the Women's Army Auxiliary Corps (WAAC) and very soon proved they could do many things not hitherto expected of them. Their dedication and bravery in dangerous and difficult situations won respect from those who had previously doubted their ability. In 1918, the women who had worked with the RFC (Royal Flying Corps) and the RNAS (Royal Naval Air Service) were invited to transfer to the WRAF (Women's Royal Air Force) when it was formed on the same day as the RAF – 1$^{st}$ April 1918.

Unfortunately, the women's service was short-lived, being disbanded two years later due to drastic post-war economy cuts. But many thousands of women remained active in the inter-war years in various voluntary organisations and associations and so were ready to serve again with the military when war in Europe once more loomed.

In September 1938 the ATS was formed; in March 1939 the WRNS. But it was not until late June 1939, a few weeks before war was declared, that the 48 RAF companies formed within the ATS, were finally separated from army administration and became the WAAF, under the directorship of Air Commandant Katherine Jane Trefusis Forbes.

At the start, entry was limited to the few trades open to women, and those were MT Driver, Equipment Assistant, Cook, Clerk and Mess staff. Soon other trades were opened to them, such as Fabric Worker, Teleprinter and Telephone Operator and Clerk/SD (Plotters).

Recruitment into the WAAF was rapid, leading to a shortage of accommodation and uniforms. Some recruits were enlisted then returned home to await call-up. Early parades saw airwomen clothed in part uniform and part civilian dress, but gradually accommodation and equipment difficulties were overcome and the girls were proud to wear the Air Force Blue. Until 1941 when the enlistment age was dropped to seventeen and a half, recruits had to be eighteen years old. Some girls, keen to be accepted, added a couple of years to their age and a few were enlisted at just sixteen years.

As time passed and confidence in WAAF ability grew, many other trades were opened to women, so that men could be released for overseas service. Group 1 technical trades were initially thought to be beyond their capabilities, but Group 2 trades were gradually opened to them, and the girls were sent on technical courses, sometimes alongside men. Some WAAFs were subjected to teasing by their counterparts in the early days, but through their diligence and capability, they were soon fully accepted and worked with airmen without resentment.

They allied themselves to the squadrons they worked on, and many were actively involved in day to day operational duties. For WAAF personnel on active fighter or bomber stations this would prove traumatic, as aircrew they had come to know were killed on flying duties. They never forgot the pain they suffered as the toll mounted.

Until the National Service Act came into force, all recruits were volunteers, but by mid-1943 womanpower was as valuable to the country in many other areas, as was manpower, and with the WAAF being a popular service, a halt to voluntary recruiting was called for, thereafter, except for a few months only, recruits were directed by National Service.

In their later years over 4,000 ex-airwomen in the United Kingdom and in overseas countries became members of the WAAF Association, in order to keep alive the friendships they shared during World War II. Through their twice-yearly magazine they were able to renew contacts with friends and comrades of their youth, enjoying monthly branch meetings and the opportunity to share recollections of wartime joy and grief, and memories of friends who had been lost.

Each year they paraded through the town that was hosting their reunion that year, and were an inspiration to many through their smart bearing, their marching ability, even those with walking sticks holding their heads high and backs straight, proud to be on parade and, as Vera Willoughby demonstrated at the reunion in Buxton in 1996, even on crutches. From all over the country they gathered together at Horseguards Parade each November to take part in the annual Parade past the Cenotaph, to show their remembrance of the airmen and airwomen they had known in the dark days of war.

The following stories of their service life were written by the women themselves, and give a vivid picture of the lives they lived then, the good days and the bad, which they all remember to this day.

**Beryl Williams, 2004**

SERVE IN THE WAAF
WITH THE MEN WHO FLY

# 1. *At Work*

## The poster that lured us

This picture has remained in the memories of a generation of women who did serve with the men who fly. The handsome couple were instrumental in the recruiting of thousands of us. They were not actors as many thought, being picked for their looks, no, they were really serving personnel. The pilot was the late Peter Parrott who, at the time the photo was taken in March 1940, was serving at Vitry-en-Artois airfield in France where he was with 607 (County of Durham) Squadron. It was featured on a poster to recruit aircrew. When later, recruiting for the WAAF was the order of the day, the original poster was altered and reissued, with A WAAF, the late Mary Scaife superimposed on it. She was later commissioned and served overseas. The two of them never met.

Peter continued his distinguished career in the RAF until 1965, when he retired as Wing Commander P.L. Parrott DFC AFC. In 1948 he married WAAF Wireless Operator Mary Dunning, who served in the Y service at RAF Chicksands.

HRH The Duchess of Gloucester, WAAF Commandant, outside Cardiff Recruiting Office, July 1942, talking with new recruits. Beryl Stephenson, 2nd from right.

# In the beginning...

RAF West Drayton was, pre-war, a reception depot for airmen. It became a depot for WAAF also in October 1939, but it was not really suitable for them, and when the air raids caused so much danger and disruption, they were moved to Harrogate in September 1940 and became No 1 WAAF Depot. They moved again to Bridgnorth at the beginning of 1941, finally closing in September 1942. No. 2 Depot opened at RAF Innsworth in January 1941. Later that year No. 3 Depot was opened at Morecambe. Whichever Depot she was drafted to, a recruit's early experience of WAAF life stayed in her memory.

At Morecambe they were billeted in the boarding houses along the front, and practiced marching and took PT in full view of residents. Innsworth was a hutted camp, and when the recruit drafts from recruit centres all over the country arrived at Gloucester Railway Station, they were gathered together by an RAF corporal who shepherded them out to an RAF bus and drove them the few miles to Innsworth. There they were faced with what appeared to be acres of brown, wooden huts which they were to learn housed offices, cookhouse, medical centre, dining room, NAAFI, cinema and sleeping quarters. A corporal counted them in 24's into a hut. They saw a row of iron beds down each side of the hut, two pot-bellied stoves, one at each end, which it was their job to keep riddled and stoked as long as they were careful with their coal ration.

On each bed were three 3 foot square mattresses, known as 'biscuits' which had to be laid along the length of the bed and four brown or grey blankets, two sheets and a round bolster-like pillow with cotton cover. The beds had to be made up each evening, and stacked every morning in regulation order, until the pile looked somewhat like a liquorice allsort.

1. Stack the 3 'biscuits' on top of each other,
2. Fold one blanket into a length that would wrap around; 1 folded blanket, 1 sheet, the second blanket, second sheet, then the third blanket.
3. Place the pile on top of biscuits, with bolster on top of the whole pile.

After this, bedspaces had to be cleaned, brushed then 'bumpered' with a heavy flannel covered brick–shaped weight on the end of a long handle until the brown lino gleamed. Then after ablutions, (sometimes a minor route march to reach these in another hut, and in winter it could still be dark when Reveille sounded.). Ablutions always seemed to smell of wet concrete, basins stretched down one side, lavatories down the other, with several baths at the end.

Back in the hut, stand by beds for the hut corporal's inspection (they encouraged competition between the huts as to which was kept the cleanest.)

Then breakfast; porridge was a staple choice. A row of cook-house girls in white overalls and caps stood behind a serving hatch, dumping out streaky bacon, fried bread or potato, or baked beans on each plate held out before them. A knife, fork and spoon had been issued to each girl who quickly learned that these important items had to be carefully looked after – no 'irons', no food. Outside each dining room was a large metal tank full of hot water for the individual washing of their 'irons'. By the time many irons had been washed, the water was not too wholesome. They found that they should pack these irons last on top of their kitbags on each subsequent posting, which invariably meant arriving at the new station during a mealtime.

During the next few days the recruits were kept busy and moving. First day it was to collect their kit from a hut that had folding tables, covered with items of clothing, stretching the length of the room. First issue was a kitbag, a long tube of white canvas with a drawstring top, a blue band around the centre. With this held open each recruit moved along as the WAAF behind each table threw items into it. They gave their sizes to the WAAF (not that this made much difference), who flung in the items, announcing as she did so, "two vests, two suspender belts, three pairs of stockings (grey lisle), three pairs of knickers (thick dark navy blue, with elasticated legs, promptly ever afterwards referred to as 'blackouts' or 'passion killers'), two brassieres, one ration bag (a white cotton drawstring bag for holding a cook-house sandwich if going on a train journey), one housewife (a 'hussif' containing needle, thread etc.), one brass button-stick with a wide slot along the centre (for sliding buttons through for polishing), gas mask, two shoe brushes, a cap, steel helmet, two pairs of shoes (black lace-ups), two skirts, two jackets, (one uniform to be kept as 'best blue', the other for work), one great-coat, one groundsheet, (to be thrown around the shoulders when it rained – not a lot of use for a tall girl, and entirely covering a short one). Coming to the end of the lineup, the girl hoisted her gas mask onto one shoulder, her kitbag onto the other, and staggered outside.

That evening and in any spare time each girl had to stitch or ink her name and number into every article of kit. She alone was responsible for its care and woe betide her if she lost anything. If it was stolen, she was still held responsible as she was required to ensure she did not leave anything around to tempt another.

A sheet of brown paper and string was issued so that civvy clothes could be packed up and sent home – thus cutting that last link with all that was familiar to them.

The following days were filled with PT sessions, lectures, drill on the parade ground, each corporal in charge determined to make her squad the best. Lectures were on RAF procedure, the dos and don'ts of service life, a talk by the WAAF CO, a slide show by the MO (giving lurid picture of the diseases that a girl could catch if she did not behave herself and caught VD. (Horrified young girls were almost put off sex for life). They were taught to salute; right arm long way up, fingers together, thumb tucked in, hand held with middle finger in line and just behind the right eye, then short way down, arm in line with skirt seam. Much practice made perfect eventually.

On church parade on their last Sunday, dressed in best blue, buttons gleaming, they were allowed out of camp for a few hours. At last the course came to an end, and postings were anxiously awaited. Would they end up near home? they wanted to know.

Those who were destined for trade training at an RAF school whether clerks S/D, F/Mechs, Cooks and so on travelled in groups to their destinations; W/Ops to Blackpool, MT drivers to Liverpool, Cooks to Melksham. Those already trained before enlisting, such as Clerk/GD, SRNs to work in Sick Quarters were posted individually, and there was sadness as they had to say goodbye to their new-found friends. Meetings and partings happened often as they later found.

They all assembled on the parade ground for the last time for their passing out parade, and the order "eyes right" was given as each squad passed before the WAAF Commanding Officer and other WAAF officers. Then it was pack kit, get up at the crack of dawn, climb aboard an RAF lorry and off to the railway station, and the journey to whatever lay before them.

# Billeted in the Workhouse

*Beryl Williams*

An immense variety of homes were requisitioned in wartime by the Air Ministry to house the increasing numbers of airmen and airwomen. Service personnel could find themselves living in a manor house in the depths of the countryside, an upmarket hotel in the West End of London, a boarding house by the seaside, or lodged with a kindly family. Or, going from the sublime to the ridiculous, huts in the middle of a muddy field (one group of these were known as 'The Piggeries'; had pigs *really* been the previous lodgers?) or an old building like the workhouse at Leighton Buzzard.

The town was home to HQ No 60 Group, Fighter Command and also the Communications Centre at RAF Stanbridge. The secret work on radar carried out at these stations was absolutely crucial to the war effort. Here also was the Plotters School and the trainees were billeted in the workhouse or in the huts in a field beyond.

Built in 1861, the building was designed to accommodate 100 men, 100 women and 60 children. The workhouse master lived in comfort in the three-storey main building. The inmates slept in very basic rooms situated in the wings that stretched out from either side of the main building and then around to enclose a square, tarmac courtyard. In the centre of the fourth wing, which faced the principle building, was an arched gatehouse. The ground floors of the two-storey wings housed store rooms; the upper floors were reached from the courtyard via two open iron staircases, one each side of the courtyard, which led up to a veranda running right around and giving access to the bedrooms used by the unfortunate derelicts. The tramps who bedded down there for the night were expected to rise at dawn to break stones in order to earn their keep, before moving on to the next town and the next workhouse.

Before the RAF could use the building for accommodation, ablutions had to be provided. A brick-built structure was erected in the courtyard with a dividing wall placed centrally inside and a door at each end: one for airmen, the other for airwomen. It was not unknown for a girl to be wallowing in the bath in her half of the building, singing her favourite aria, to find herself drawn into a duet by a male voice coming through the wall from the other half! If a visit to the ablutions was required late at night, it meant a dark and chilly traipse, hoping it wasn't raining, along the veranda, down the open staircase, across the courtyard ... and then the whole journey in reverse.

An artist's impression of the Workhouse.

One dark and rainy night, a distracted swan landed in the courtyard, having mistaken the gleam of the wet tarmac for water, and was unable to take off again. It was a brave girl who would ignore the flapping of wings and ominous hisses to cross in darkness to the ablutions. (The RSPCA were soon sent for. They captured the bird and drove it to the nearest stretch of open water.)

The building was officially named and always referred to as 'the PLI' (Poor Law Institute), which led to much hilarity when telling friends where one was billeted.

The school is well remembered by the hundreds of Clerk/SD/Plotters who trained there. They were marched each day for practical training to the Communications Centre at RAF Stanbridge, which was able to operate if the Ops room at Bentley Priory was put out of action. The painted and camouflaged netting which covered the station made the girls feel they were, like the children of Hamelin, disappearing into a green hill.

The workhouse was only one of many varieties of wartime billets, and apart from that one, Derry Bourne's tally was a stable, an orphanage, two village halls, an underground GCI bunker, assorted huts, a teacher training college, a chateau and the bombed half of a convent. From the ridiculous to the sublime would you say?

# The Parachute Packers

*Beryl Williams*

To 'fly through the air like a bird' was the dream of men for centuries, and strange contraptions were made in their endeavours to achieve this dream. For centuries also, their thoughts had turned to inventing a device to carry them safely to earth from a great height. Early designs of these made of some unlikely materials looked odd, though intrepid inventors used them, unfortunately not always successfully. When the Chinese discovered the art of weaving silk from the cocoon of a little worm, they had found the ideal material – light and flexible but strong. Some of the earliest recorded descents were made from hot air balloons, though insufficient height was reached to avoid some disastrous landings. The first descent in England was in 1810.

In England, development of the parachute intensified after WW1, due in part to the indignation of the public on learning that the German Air Force had made a general issue of chutes to their airmen during the later stages of that war, but the RFC did not, and consequently many airmen who might have been saved had lost their lives. Different types of chutes were tested, but the Irvin parachute was the one adopted by the RAF. This was made in USA by the company founded by Leslie Irvin, who then formed a company in England (named Irvine by mistake) and who, incidentally, became the driving force behind the Caterpillar Club (the idea of two newspaper men in 1922). During World War II Irvin was to award thousands of golden caterpillar brooches to applicant aircrew who had baled out from an aircraft emergency. Some POWs in Germany applied successfully for their brooches, and these were sent to their homes to await their eventual release. Airborne forces, however, were not eligible, as their parachute descents were premeditated, not the result of emergencies.

The folding and packing of a parachute was absolutely critical to its success, and skill was required for this operation. From 1941 onwards, many WAAF were trained in this skill, and aircrew, airborne troops and SOE agents regarded these girls with gratitude and respect. A parachuting padre confessed, after making his first jump from a balloon during his training, that all his life he had placed his entire trust in God, but for the time it took for his parachute to open, his confidence was transferred to a young airwoman parachute packer. Another story goes that aircrew passing a parachute packing section were warned not to look through the windows and distract the girls as, 'they could be packing your parachute'.

Until 1943, when nylon was increasingly being used, a parachute was made from 60 yards of silk, divided into 96 panels (which made it stronger than if in one piece, and easier to replace a damaged part).

The packing room had to be spotlessly clean, the temperature even and the air dry, as any damp would mean vital seconds of delay when the parachute opened. After use it was hung from the ceiling for drying and uncreasing before being laid out and repacked at the three foot wide, long tables and used again. Each chute was inspected and repacked regularly, and used for 25 descents only. (Old parachutes were highly sought after for making into ladies' undies and even wedding dresses.) The history of each was kept in a log book by the packers, and the name of the packer of each was recorded against the ones she packed. Notices hanging from the ceiling warned – REMEMBER, A MAN'S LIFE DEPENDS ON EVERY PARACHUTE YOU PACK. But they were hardly necessary as the girls were well aware that a man's life depended on their skill, asking themselves if they would trust their own lives to their packing. A packer at Ringway wrote a moving poem on the feelings she had over her work and this is reproduced.

There were different ways of packing to be learned, depending on whether it was a seat, back, chest, lap or training chute. When folded and packed into their haversacks, the webbing stitched, and the chute ready for use, the weight was approximately equal to eleven 2lb bags of sugar. Other types, used to drop supplies to the SOE, the Maquis, or to the airborne troops on the ground, were coloured, each colour, red, yellow, bright blue denoting a different item of equipment, ranging from rations, weapons, vehicles, medical supplies and various other needs.

**Kathleen Chapple (now Sainsbury)** was stationed at Netheravon in 1943-44 where all helped towards the success of the paratroop landings in Normandy. Kath was in charge of the repair section where pilots' parachutes were white silk, and the paratroops used camouflaged chutes. She was sent to St Athan to learn about the quick release box, worn by the troops on their harness, enabling them to unharness quickly once they had landed. They had many visits from members of the Royal family who were interested in the girls' work.

Parachutes have undergone developments in design and fabric since the war. The faster jets and consequent fierce windblast caused great difficulties for crew having to escape, and as early as 1946 ejection seats were being tested, with the pilot being shot into the air in his seat, with the parachute opening automatically

Kathleen (Betty) Pemble, Canterbury, trained at Wilmslow and then was posted first to Sutton Bridge, then Credenhill for an eight week SEA course where she learned how to pack parachutes and dinghies. On her passing out test she says;

I was given a pilot's parachute – with the rip cords twisted – to pack, but although hectic, I managed it. I was then posted to Waltham, near Grimsby and joined No. 100 Squadron (Lancasters) Bomber Command, where I packed the parachutes with Terry Wardle and Ethel Sykes. We looked after the crews chutes and they were great with us.

When not in use, we hung the parachutes in the section at a certain temperature, and packed the others at a long table. The pack and the chutes were laid out and folded in place, kept by bean bags. We threaded nylon cord in and out of the loops inside the pack, making sure that they pulled out easily if needed. Then the chutes were folded and put into the pack, fixing the auxiliary chute in last. Then the pack folded and the rip cord handle fixed. The observers wore their packs on the chest, so if they had to bale out they pulled the rip cord handle to release the chute. Of course the pilots had to sit on their packs, but their rip cord handle was attached to the front of the harness and was still easy to pull.

I was known then as 'Betty' and one day a letter came from the parents of a crew member thanking 'Betty in Parachute Section' for saving his life when he baled out at 500 feet over the coast of Norway. Unfortunately I wasn't able to keep the letter, as it was put with the papers of the section.

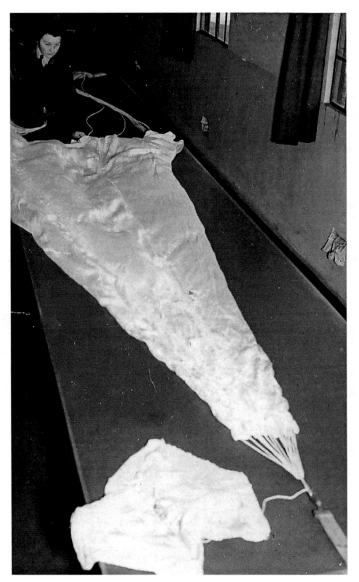

Parachute ready to be packed.

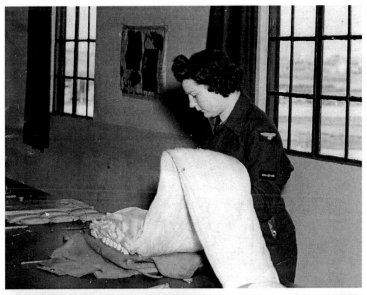

A WAAF parachute packer at work.

# If you can stand the first fortnight...

*Edna Murray née Gulley*

I was told if you can stand the first fortnight in the WAAF you will enjoy it. How right they were. I volunteered in March 1941, and after surviving Innsworth, was posted to RAF Feltwell, a bomber station. As an Equipment Assistant my job was to check and list the personal effects of the brave boys who hadn't returned from missions. Although as my first posting, it was exciting but it was also harrowing, particularly if I knew the men who were missing. One squadron based there was a New Zealand squadron, No. 75, and little did I know then that in the future I would myself be in the Royal New Zealand Air Force.

After several courses I was posted to Aldergrove and Castle Archdale in Northern Ireland. I loved the country and the people, and, being in Coastal Command we were near the loughs where the seaplanes were based.

At Castle Archdale I was the corporal 'Store Basher' in the Marine Section which involved checking inventories on the Air/Sea Rescue launches on Lough Erne. What a lovely job on a bright, sunny morning. I spent a total of three years in Ulster and can say it was an interesting and lovely experience.

I was posted to Stanmore where I travelled in and around London in a removal van which had been converted into a mobile clothing van, visiting balloon barrage sites. It was heartbreaking to see the devastation caused by bombs.

In 1945 I volunteered for overseas service and was posted to Algiers. Only a small contingent went, in order to take over airmen's duties so that they could be demobbed. We lived in the St George Hotel, and were transported daily to a Maintenance Unit on the beach.

After a year we all left Algiers and were flown by Dakota to Egypt, touching down at Castle Benito for an overnight stop for refuelling and so on. The station was all male, and on seeing about 20 WAAF arrive they quickly organised a dance. What a night it was! A concrete floor, hundreds of partners, every dance an 'excuse me' and the only place found for us to sleep in was in sick quarters, where we were locked in.

I came home in 1947, but after a period in 'civvy street' my wanderlust returned and I joined the RNZAF.

# WAAF Friendships

*Jackie Rawlings née Wain*

I was delighted to read two reports on the duties of Clerks/SD, which brought back happy memories of my time in the Ops Room attached to RAF Turnhouse, and later at the Radar Ops Room at Drem, with four, then six very special friends.

Four other prospective Clerks/SD and I first met at Morecambe railway station when, at the end of square bashing, we were posted, not to the area of our choice (Southern England) but to Scotland! With a corned beef sandwich as sustenance for the day, we were on the best of terms by the time we reached Carlisle, where we had to change trains. Here we were given a slip of paper with the name of the station where we should alight. We had not heard of this place before and we leaned out of the train window to listen to the name at every tiny station we stopped at, checking it against the name on the paper. Clearly we were in a foreign country! Eventually, after rejecting yet another strange name, we were startled to hear a voice call out to the station master, 'Stop the train! There should be five WAAF on board.'

As we got out, dragging our kit-bags, the station master was saying, 'Och, hurry up ye stupid wee lassies!'

A boys' prep school in the village of Dalmeny was our billet, and the admin sergeant assured us we would find plenty of baths on the floor to which we were assigned.

Washing kit in hand we went in search and were abashed to find only a very large room with about a dozen baths lined around three of its sides. We, that is Myrtle Smith, Joan Osborne, 'Little' Eileen, Sheila and I agreed now was no time for modesty. With no hooks available, we each made a neat pile of clothes, towel on top, on the floor at the end of our chosen bath as the lovely hot water filled them. We laughed and joked as we bathed and when finished, stood up and pulled out the plugs...

Aghast, we watched as our clothes were swept away on a tide of soapy water. We hadn't noticed that none of the baths were individually plumbed and all the water flowed across a slightly sloping floor to a drain in the centre of the room. Horror soon turned to laughter.

The five of us were on B watch with three equally rookie airmen, under the fatherly eye of Corporal 'Sandy'. We soon grew accustomed to the Scots accent coming to us through our earphones from the intrepid Observer Corps personnel who had to cope in all weathers while we were safe, warm and dry in the Ops Room.

'Big' Eileen joined us after a while and was later posted with us to the Radar Ops Room at Drem where we were joined by Katy, a rosy-faced girl from Devon. There was never a cross word between us and I was sad to say goodbye to all but Katy when she and I were posted to the Ops room at No. 11 Group HQ. However, while 'signing in' we took advantage of a call over the tannoy for volunteers to join SHAEF (though Katy did not later go to France with me). My work at Stanmore, Versailles and eventually Frankfurt, consisted of keeping record of available aircrew and aircraft from pre D-Day to the final victory.

Wherever I went in the WAAF I had very happy times with wonderful friends. I hope that someone from those days will also remember me.

Where Next? Drawn by Betty Turner

# What would we have done without the NAAFI?

We could buy postage stamps at the NAAFI, writing paper, shoe polish and Brasso for our buttons. At a break time we could keep ourselves going with 'tea and a wad', a sticky bun, a rock cake or some other filling goodie. (As we worked and played hard and were always hungry, we really needed filling.) Evenings on camp could be spent inside in the warm, listening to music if anyone could be persuaded to play the piano, or just relaxing and chatting together. For the airmen, the NAAFI van was a welcome sight when it arrived out at the flights with the inevitable tea and 'wad'. If the weather outside was wet and cold, the glad cry of 'NAAFI up!' warmed their spirits. NAAFI personnel served overseas, on ships or wherever there were service personnel needing their expertise. They faced the same dangers as their clients, some of them earning decorations for bravery and their dedicated service. We owe them so much. The cartoon below says it all.

Cartoon: from Naafi Up! AQ & DJ Publications 1996.

*GI to Naafi girl in uniform:* What service are you in honey?
*Naafi girl:* Navy, Army and Air Force Institute.
*GI:* Gee honey, you can't be in all three of 'em!

# The Jankers Queen

*By Molly Barker*

Not all WAAF were smart, punctual on duty or back from weekend pass or leave when they should have been, or perhaps had lost some item of kit, and couldn't account for it on kit inspections. Punishment for these petty misdeeds came swiftly, with girls being 'put on charge' and marched between two escorts (hats off in case it was used as a missile), as Molly Baker explains in her poem:

I'm up on a fizzer tomorrow,
They call me the Jankers Queen;
I'll be back peeling spuds in the cookhouse,
And all of you know what that means.

I have to report 09.00
Promptly at Station HQ
With buttons and shoes brightly polished,
Smart as paint in my very best blue.

I'll stand in the corridor waiting
Between two gynormous SPs,
While one of them says to the other
"Is she standing or still on her knees?"

The WAAF Admin Sergeant will bellow
"Left right – at the double –left, right!"
And I'll be wheeled in before the Queen Bee
An awesome and terrible sight.

Then, "Hats off!" she'll roar and say "Please Ma'am,
This airwoman here's on a charge";
Then "Fall in and stand to attention!"
(That last bit to me from the Sarge.)
I know what will happen precisely

It's happened so often before
And I'm sure some of you will remember
Your King's Regulations and more

The Corporal SP produces
A notebook and chants "I believe
This 'airwoman 'ere has been AWOL
And late coming back from 'er leave.

I tried to explain what had happened
When the SP on duty yelled "Halt!"
My train had been stopped in an air raid,
And really it wasn't my fault.

Ma'am fixes on me looks of loathing
"An utter disgrace to the WAAF
What have you to say?" - It's so childish
I just have to stand there and laugh.

At this the WAAF G turns bright purple
And screams, "Sergeant take her and go
I don't intend dealing with this one
I'm sending her to the C.O."

Then he, poor chap, tries to look solemn
And dredge up a hard, steely gaze
"I have no choice and must award you
Confinement to camp, fourteen days."

I had thought an award – like a medal,
Was something of which to be proud
But fourteen days jankers? AWARDED?
I ask you? For crying out loud!

The system was crazy in some ways

But then I suppose that it's fate.
You're of age to defend King and Country
But too young to be two minutes late.

23.59 my pass said,
And really, when all's said and done
The air-raid had done me no favours
I reached camp at 00.01.

You'll recall that, when busy with jankers,
You reported each hour on the dot
At Admin, in best bib and tucker
And here's where the Air Force got caught.

Escape routes from camp sites were easy,
And friends would be waiting for you
At 22.00 when finished
And already clad in best blue.

With some sort of organised transport
If only your old issue bike
No matter! The boyfriend was waiting
And romance was ready to strike.

So I'm up on a fizzer tomorrow
But fourteen days wont get *me* down'
For when it's gone 22.00
I'm off to a dance in the town!

# The Filter Room

*Moira Pearson née McCrudden and ex-Corporal Felicity Ashbee*

The following account of work in the Filter Room was the combined effort of LACW Moira Pearson née McCrudden, 422172 and Corporal Felicity Ashbee 885360. Later, Felicity was commissioned, and in 1943 Moira became a Sergeant Watchkeeper in Bomber Command, ending up with 617 Squadron at Coningsby.

When I joined up in 1940, after drilling and being kitted out at Harrogate, I was sent with fourteen other WAAF to Leighton Buzzard to do our training as Clerks/SD (Special Duties). We were soon to find out what 'special' duties meant for us! We learned the rudiments of plotting on the national grid and received lectures on radar, or RDF (Radio Direction Finding) as it was then called. At the end of our course we were sent to Fighter Command Filter Operations – five of us to Preston (9 Group), five to Bath (10 Group), and I was among the lucky five to be sent to HQ Fighter Command at Stanmore (11 Group).

Fighter Command Headquarters was housed at Bentley Priory, a converted mansion where Nelson once flirted with Emma Hamilton. Our filter room was sixty feet below ground and at the entrance we were challenged by a guard to show our passes. We were very proud of the fact that our job was one of the best kept secrets of the war. We had, of course, signed the Official Secrets Act. Here we worked a 24-hour watch system, working four hours at a time. Next door to us was the Ops Room where the plotters, with their magnetic rods, received information from us and plotted aircraft activities over land. We plotted surface craft and the aircraft over the sea.

Our plotting room in 1940 showed the coastline only, from Scotland down the English coast around Kent and along the

Channel to Land's End, and took in the opposite coasts of France, the Netherlands and Denmark, right up to the northernmost part of Norway, all of which gradually became enemy-occupied territory.

Each WAAF was known by the name of her station and wore headphones plugged in with telephonic connection to Dover or Pevensey, Rye, Ventnor and so on around the South and East coast. The WAAF or airman at the radar post gave Stanmore plotters the necessary information as it showed up. The radar post was often just a mobile van in some quiet meadow near the sea.

On the balcony in the Filter Room sat the controller who had direct telephone communication with each plotter and each radar station. Near him on either side of the balcony were the Liaison Officers of both Army and Navy. The Army Officer controlled air raid warnings and the Navy looked after all shipping, so all three services played their part from the balcony above the plotters. Every hour the tellers (when time permitted) would give to the Ops room and all the Sector Fighter stations the latest convoy positions. Convoys all had code names and I well remember the Controller calling from the balcony, "Bottom, remove Bottom from the table". This caused some amusement.

Each plotter at the table had a tray of coloured tiddly winks or counters numbered 1-5. As the WAAF received the information from radar she plotted on the grid reference given – for 2½ minutes with No. 1 counter, 2½ minutes with No. 2 and so on, up to the fifth counter. Every station colour was different and we were guided by a clock on the wall indicating the colour changes through the hour.

The Filter Room at Bentley Priory, 1941

When the tracks started, Filter Officers at several positions around the table would place arrows on the aircraft track made by these plots. Small trays were placed showing each track's information with the identification, height and number of aircraft. This information was phoned through to the Ops plotters in the next room and to all the Fighter Sector stations by the tellers who sat at three different positions on the balcony.

By about 1942/3 the table had to be changed. It was necessary to concentrate our efforts on the South of England. That was when Inverness, Watnell near Nottingham and Belfast opened. At this time Stanmore Filter had to work operationally from Leighton Buzzard where a copy of our new table had been constructed.

All this I seem to remember, came about in time for the Blitz. When going on watch at 9.00 pm you would be working non-stop, with only a 10 minute break, both plotting or telling until you were relieved at 1am. During that time the tellers would keep up an almost uninterrupted sing-song litany of grid references, numbers of aircraft and height... "W for Willie, X for X-ray 4257 4257 15 plus at 10, W for Willie, N for Nuts 2149, 2149 11 plus at 15..." At times like these the balcony would serve as a lookout area and would suddenly and quietly fill with 'top brass' – high ranking officers and VIPs who had come to get a picture of the extent of the raid. One regularly spotted famous faces – the King, Winston Churchill and so on. Nobody stopped work, of course, and it was the one time we did not stand to attention!

In conclusion, I should mention the Observer Corps, who regularly did such valuable service to the RAF, giving accurate sightings of enemy aircraft.

# A Plotter at Uxbridge

*Ruby Sladen née Hall*

No. 4 Watch was a happy group, hostile tracks were being plotted at the time the photograph was taken. The majority of us were together for three years and were usually on duty when VIPs, such as Winston Churchill paid us a visit.

Most of the Battle of Britain pilots would do a session of controlling in the Ops Room, then go back to their Sectors. We were on night duty for the commencement of the D-Day invasion and were not allowed out of camp the previous evening. We were told to rest as something would be happening during the night. Because we were spending so much time 'down the hole' sun-ray treatment was compulsory twice a week, the sun-ray lamp had been provided by Lord Nuffield.

We had some very interesting people working with us, including three film stars: Rex Harrison, Cyril Raymond and Ronald Adam. I can still hear Rex Harrison's squeaky voice saying "Who has the gin bottle?" at the get-together in the office en route to the Christmas camp dance.

After night duty a tracing of the night's activity had to be taken to GC Night Ops, at one time it was "Cats Eyes" Cunningham and everyone wanted to take it. Because we were on duty so many hours a day we had a 56-hour pass every week. This enabled my friend and me to hitch lifts to Gloucester and home.

Uxbridge being the end of the tube line meant we had easy access to and from London, so were able to take advantage of the free tickets for the shows, which continued to run all through the war. We would pick up the tickets from the cabin in Leicester Square and, being fussy, did not just take the first show offered to us.

The Ops Room, Uxbridge. Photo: Courtesy, IWM London Ref. CH 7698.

# Impressions of Operations

*Hester Parrington (now Smallbone), RAF Digby, May 1943.*

Cool, pastel shades
Of beige and green
Dark brown polished floor,
White unrelenting light
And colour in bright splashes
Round the plotting tables
Where arrows lie in trays
Red – yellow – blue
Tricolour tracks
Across a pale green sea
And vivid lettered plaques
Telephones always humming
Messages always coming
Aircraft always flying
And men sometimes dying
Strange code words
And a pilot's voice
Over the radio telephone
Calling his base
Always calling
Always answered

Far away
The unseen watchers of the ether
Sense a reverberation
And simultaneously
This tremulous flicker
Across a lucent screen

Becomes a hostile track
Moving across the sea
And there on the painted table
A battle rages
A man dies…
An enemy perhaps, but still a man
And the sea, all embracing
Enfolds him in her bosom
At rest. While
Weaving erratic tracks
Across the squares
Our fighters wing back
From their mission of destruction
Calling their base
in victory.

And still I feel
How weird, fantastic
Is this children's play
Of coloured counters
Arrow, discs and plaques
Symbolic travesty
Of human life.
So may the gods themselves
Look down and laugh
In careless incredulity
At this fresh testament
To Man's insanity.

Clerks Special Duties always had a good press, and rightly so, their work on the plotting tables was important and fired the imagination of journalists. But of equal importance to the well-being of RAF men and women was the more humble work of those who laboured in the cookhouse and kept the air force fed. This work was hard, hot and repetitive, but the girls who worked in the various messes were proud of the service they gave. Two cooks tell of their work in the cookhouse, below.

## A Cook's Tour

*Kathleen Mackenzie née Hall*

In 1940 at Croydon I enlisted after being bombed out of my home in Peckham, London. I had spent three years at a catering college hoping to make a career of cooking, so it was my first choice of trade; also I had been told that cooks were desperately needed as no-one seemed to want to go into this trade.

Within two weeks of joining I was on my way to Melksham and then to Morecambe for square bashing. Then to the cookery school at Cosford for three weeks and a posting afterwards to the Officers Mess at North Luffenham. I had quite a shock on seeing the kitchen there after the fairly modern one at Cosford with their very good ovens. This kitchen was small, and had a red quarry tiled floor which became very slippery if anything was spilled on it. Cooking was done on two coal-fired ranges, one of which was also kept well stoked up and only used when the other needed stoking. This took quite a while to get used to.

There were nine WAAF and two sergeant cooks during the daytime, plus one GD (General Duties), usually an airman waiting for a trade course. While I was there, the GD was waiting for an Air Mechanics course, and he eventually became my husband.

The sergeant cooks ruled us with a rod of iron as they were not too happy at having WAAF cooks in the kitchen. Incidentally they never worked the night shifts. The girls worked three shifts, 6am-2pm, 2pm-10pm and 10pm-6am. The night shift was the most stressful. We were miles from anywhere and any strange noise seemed worse than it was.

Kathleen in 1942

On night shift we had to peel by hand a very large bin of potatoes ready for the day shift, and when there were flying operations, we had a certain number of breakfasts to cook when the crews returned. This wasn't too bad until you got to the last two or three plates and you knew then that some planes were overdue.

I really enjoyed my life at North Luffenham and still hope that one day I will be lucky enough to go back and see how the kitchen compares with the one I worked in, and whether the WAAF quarters are still there,. And I wonder if the hole made in the hedge by some of the WAAF who met their boyfriends and sneaked in after curfew, is also still there...

# Like Jankers Every Day

*Violet Holden née Carpenter*

I joined the WAAF in 1942 and became a cook, which was my own choice after learning that mess staff were desperately needed. After routine procedure at Innsworth, kitting up, jabs and so on, I went on a three-month course to Cosford. Here we had to learn tasks like boning a full side of bacon (I had only seen rashers previously) – and woe betide you if there was any meat left on the bone after finishing! An unpleasant job was rendering down all available bits of fat in three boilers (nothing was wasted); they had to be constantly stirred to avoid burning. This became known as 'the sweat room' as a whole day in there was like a sauna!

After learning other cookery skills besides slicing hundreds of rashers and making as many meals, I was sent to Liverpool on a 'Cooking for Officers' course. This, to me, was farcical; stuffed tomatoes was just one of the many daft items we had to cook. Thank goodness I ended up in the Sergeants Mess!

After passing my exams I was promoted to LACW and given a menu book entitled 'RAF Book of Cooking and Dietary'. It sounds grand for 1942 and I still have that book but the menu quantities are for 100 men (not much use for a family of four!).

My first station was RAF Blackbrook. The kitchen here was basic; any mixtures were put into a large wooden trough and two girls would begin to mix by hand. Still, only about 150 personnel were at this station.

Next came 214 Squadron at RAF Oulton. Here we had a more modern kitchen, which was needed with twice as many men to feed. There were large boilers for cooking vegetables; we got burned stomachs and feet often when emptying or cleaning these monsters. Also there was a large Hobart mixer I used. One day we were running late with the meal. 'Sarge' called to me to hurry with the veg, which was already in the mixer. I ran and pressed a button and suddenly there was veg flying everywhere! I had pushed the wrong speed switch. That was one of my bad days…

We cooked pies and sweets in tins and trays about two and a half feet square and they were quite heavy to carry when full and hot. This was when we welcomed the bad boys on 'jankers' who were sent to the kitchen for punishment. Funny that; we girls must have been on jankers for years!

In my four years as a cook I never heard any complaints about the food; the only grouse was quantity, and there were always requests for "any seconds, Love?" But of course we were rationed, just like civilians, with maybe a little extra.

All mess staff had a good sense of humour and we could still laugh after a hard day and a long ride on those awful bikes back to the billet down narrow rough roads – worse still when the 'Forts' (Flying Fortresses) were returning; their backdraft could send you and your bike back to the mess!

On demob my discharge papers gave me a glowing reference as a cook … but no way did I want to see the inside of a kitchen for a very long time.

The Mess staff at RAF Blackbrook.

Cooks learning to use outdoor equipment somewhere in England.

# Memories of Dyce & Aberdeen

*Margaret Poole née Marchant*

I was stationed at Bridlington on the Yorkshire coast, the nearest I'd ever been posted to my home town of Bradford, when I was told I'd been posted to Dyce, near Aberdeen. Quite exciting, as I'd never been to Scotland before, but I had many dire warnings:

"It's a little fishing village miles from anywhere…"

"They don't like the English…"

"It snows in summer…"

So it was with some trepidation that I took the train at York for the very long journey. Travelling on a long distance train was an adventure in itself, always very crowded with all three services and many from the Empire, as it was then. But as many will know, wartime comradeship and spirit were abundant. I remember that after embarking at York there were no vacant seats so I sat on the toilet lid for some hours, with two soldiers on the floor and an airman nonchalantly leaning against the door, having long discussions about whether the Tay Bridge would repeat the disaster of many years previously when we passed over.

My first impression of Aberdeen I well remember; no-one had told me that it was known as 'the granite city'. It was a beautiful, sunny, blue-skied day and the sight of the gleaming granite shining in the sun is one I will never forget. In fact the almost two years I spent at Dyce, with many visits to my 'gleaming city' were perhaps the most happy in my service.

As for what I'd been told, "They're all very mean" etc – it was, in fact, difficult to walk down Union Street at any time without a civilian stopping and asking me to join them for tea, supper or a 'dram'. The only time I ever found any inkling for the reputation was when I went out to tea one day and on being offered a scone, jam and butter, put both on the scone. The conversation stopped, and I realised it was *either* jam *or* butter, but not both.

There was a large contingent of WAAF at Dyce and I like to think that we were all happy and contented. The Canadian Forestry Corps were stationed in the Grampians and invited the WAAF to their social evenings. The journey was quite a long way into the hills in an old RAF bus. Being the Flight Sergeant in charge of the airwomen who went was quite hair-raising. Assisted by a WAAF Sergeant Everett, trying to keep young airwomen from the temptation of succumbing to the wiles of wild Canadian soldiers, who desperately plied them with unmentionable drinks before whisking them away to the woods – to presumably show them their forestry skills – was something that I laugh about in retrospect, but at the time was quite alarming. The head count for the departure bus was very worrying!

I've never been back to Aberdeen, but would love to go one day for two reasons: first, to see the sea – the coast was out of bounds in the war and I never did go there. Secondly, I would like to go to the police station in Union Street. I can't remember why, but I missed the last bus back to camp one night. I couldn't afford a hotel, so asked a policeman if he could help me. He could, and took me to the police station and offered me a cell; very comfortable too, with extra blankets and a cup of tea in the morning! The Sergeant told me that he would have to enter me in the books as a vagrant, and he did. If they still have the records I'd love to see the entry.

I left my lovely city for Blackpool and a different way of life. All experience and education, though I'm afraid I didn't appreciate it at the time.

# A Batwoman at War

*Pat Woodyatt née Smith*

At RAF Bridgenorth in August 1941 I was asked on interview what work I had done before enlisting. I told the WAAF officer that my Dad had not let me go out to work as my Mum had died when I was twelve years old. I had to take care of Dad and my three brothers until they were called up into the army. The officer said, "Good. You will make a good batwoman."

And so I did. I loved the work and took great pride in it.

The day began by taking morning tea to the officers and collecting their uniforms and shoes to clean and polish. After breakfast we batwomen would make beds and clean rooms. If the officers needed their uniforms pressed they would ask us to do this too ... but they never failed to say 'thank you' or show appreciation.

One night a week we worked 'reception duty' – showing incoming officers to their quarters, supplying their rooms with fresh drinking water, closing curtains and turning back bedclothes etc.

At 9 Group HQ Fighter Command, Barton Hall in 1943, our RAF officers were billeted at Newsome House, a huge place, with quite a number of resting officers, some from Middle East Command and other ex-Battle of Britain pilots. One of my favourites was Flying Officer Michael Bentine, later to be famous on television. I remember him well. He wore shoulder flashes emblazoned with B.L.A.V. (British Latin American Volunteers). My friend and I thought he was a royal prince and didn't know if we should curtsy or bow, but he quickly put us at ease. He was extremely handsome, most kind, just one year older than myself. He was clever at languages and painstakingly taught me to sing 'On the Bridge of Avignon' in French. We met again some years later when he appeared at The Grand Theatre in Wolverhampton, and I was thrilled to see him. He was still so very kind and thoughtful.

When news came of the D-Day invasion, things began to alter quickly. We were posted to Barton Grange to look after WAAF officers – a big change for us, but just as pleasant, all grateful for whatever we did for them and it was nice to be appreciated. I still remember their names.

I was then posted to RAF Halfpenny Green, where I was honoured to become batwoman to the station padre, Reverend Proctor VC.[1]

---

[1] A.H. Proctor was awarded the V.C. in August 1916 while serving as a private with the King's (Liverpool) Regiment. He was ordained in 1927 and died in 1973. A memorial to him is in Sheffield Cathedral.

# Serving with the Dambusters

*Morfydd Jane Brooks (ACW Gronland née Rose)*

My first glimpse of RAF Scampton filled me with deepest gloom. It was a raw, windy day in March 1943 when I with five other WAAF huddled together in the back of an RAF van and trundled into the camp. As we passed the huge hangars we could see on the runways the shapes of five Lancaster aircraft. I was glad I was a WAAF and wouldn't have to fly them.

On parade next morning a young Pilot Officer welcomed all the new arrivals and told us about the new squadron. It was being formed for a very special operation which had to be kept a complete secret, and whatever information we might overhear in the course of our duties was not to be repeated. He told us our Squadron Commander's name was Guy Gibson, and warned us to be particular about our dress because the commander was a stickler for neatness.

Three of us were sent to the Sergeants Mess. Our duties were light; we laid tables, served food to the aircrews; then cleaned up and made ourselves useful. Mealtimes were adjusted to suit training schedules. Whatever time the crews arrived, there would always be a hot meal ready – 'for they were the warriors'.

We heard the planes land, then the doors would burst open and the aircrew would swarm in, shouting boisterously as we served their meals. We young WAAF had to endure a barrage of good-natured banter, such as: "I dreamed of you all night" – "Serve us in the nude" – or one of them would ask, "What's the collective noun for WAAF?"

"A Mattress of WAAF!" they would all reply.

We took it all in good part because we knew the great strain they were under and the danger they would face.

Sometimes, while out on a date, they would wonder about their probable targets, ships, submarine pens or dams, so when told their targets on 15th May they were not altogether surprised.

When they emerged from their briefing conference they looked grim and strained, all the banter was silenced. We tried to jolly them up, but to no avail. All that day and the next they were taken up in feverish activity. Aircraft were checked and rechecked, wireless equipment tested and guns and the famous 'bouncing bombs' loaded.

Late evening on the 16th May they were ready to go. All WAAF and ground crew watched the great planes prepare to depart. We watched with heavy hearts because we knew that many of our friends would never return. To worsen our fears we had been told that Guy Gibson's dog had been knocked down and killed. A very bad omen.

The first wave sped down the runway and headed south, quickly followed by the second, then the last four back-up planes. We stood silently until the sound of their engines had died away, then drifted back to our duties. There was no sleep for anyone that night, our minds were on those aircraft. Twice we heard engines and rushed outside. The WAAF sergeant tried to calm us and made us coffee.

Some time later we heard in the far distance the sounds we had been waiting for and ran to the landing strips to see the planes land. We were ordered back to the mess to serve the first arrivals, but no aircrew came in. Two hours later the sergeant called us together and told us the sad news that of our nineteen aircraft, only eleven had returned. Fifty-six of our young boys would never return. We burst into tears as we looked around at the tables we had laid. They looked so empty and pathetic.

The following few days were a nightmare; we were shattered by the terrible loss and although we gradually began to adjust to squadron routine, nothing could ever be the same again.

In the course of the next few months, many of us were posted to different squadrons and were told that the 'higher-ups' thought we had become too involved with the aircrews to function efficiently. I think they were right.

---

Morfydd worked in the Bridgend Arsenal until joining the WAAF, which she did when her husband, whom she had met at the arsenal, joined the RAF. She became a waitress after being called 'a barrage balloon reject' by a sergeant!

---

# Once and Forever

*Dorothy Gray née Whyte, ex-WAAF corporal.*

Do you recall the flying boats that flew from Oban Bay?
The spinning wave, the roar that sent an echo through the dawn,
The flashing lamp, a hand that waved, the long slow rise that curved?
Ah, all of that, my love, is gone as is our yesterday.

The fliers back, their sheepskins huddled into, stiff with cold,
Their voices, laughter as they spoke, reports to make and file,
The faces lined with weariness yet still young and full of hope,
A convoy safely into port where a matelot's tale grows bold.

The months they flew, my love, the years they went to mark our life,
The fogs, the rain, the winds that blew like knives from out the North,
I hear it still, that roar that went an echoing down the loch,
In dreams, in memories still, my love, of that long vanished strife.

The bay is quiet now, my love, its yachts are bright and gay.
And children play where once a plane lay shattered on the strand,
And where the Aldis flashed its light and gunfire rattled sharp
But, ah, my love, all that is just our long-gone yesterday.

# From Oily Rag to Flight Mechanic

*Pat Tasker née Stocking*

My road to becoming a Flight Mechanic was not straightforward. It was necessary to volunteer for a completely different trade. The RAF was nothing if not contrary!

I was sent to Hednesford after the customary 'square bashing' in Morecambe (I often wonder if the sight of us in our knickers doing PT stunted the growth of those awestruck children who always watched us!). At Hednesford I met a group of equally bewildered WAAF, none of whom knew anything about mechanics. To say we were welcomed would not be correct, we were, of course, entering a previously all-male preserve, but they were stuck with us and were somewhat patronisingly surprised when we passed our tests some four months later.

I was then sent to Cranfield in the company of a girl named Dot. We were the first WAAF Flight Mechanics they had ever seen. They were neither expecting us nor did they really want us. For a few months we were sent for tea, oily rags, etc, not let near the planes and had to suffer remarks like "Powder its nose, lovey," … but slowly we earned our spurs.

Being a Flight Mech was never the most popular trade; we smelled of petrol and oil, even after a bath, and took our meals at all sorts of odd hours because our work took place mainly on the 'Flights', some three miles from the main camp, reached by bicycle in all weathers.

It was our job to make sure the aircraft were safe to fly – oil, petrol, air pressure, brakes, etc – also to test run the engines… One day I stupidly decided that I couldn't be bothered to cross the field to pick up chocks before revving a Spitfire's engine (a cardinal sin) and found myself taxiing gently towards a line of parked aircraft… I cannot repeat what my Flight Sergeant said!

# A 'Grease Monkey' Remembers

*'Ginger' Parkinson (now Eileen Ramsay)*

There were two sections, Flight Mechanic/Engines and Flight Mechanic/Airframes or 'grease monkeys' as we were often called. After three weeks square bashing I was sent on a four month course, two to Innsworth and two to Halton.

Then I worked on Oxfords on 'minor inspections' and Harvards on 'daily inspections'. On minor inspections (after 40 hours of flying) we worked in the hangars with an engine each to service in one day. We had set hours, 08.30-17.00 hours, with one and a half hours for lunch. On Harvards we just had to refuel, start them up, and see there were no leaks or anything dropping off. We signed for everything and now and again one of us had to go on the test flight.

The airmen used to play tricks on us. Once I was sent from one hangar to the next to ask for 'a Long Stand' until 'Lofty' in the stores told me it was a joke. We took these pranks in good humour and I enjoyed my three and a half years in the WAAF.

# My War as a Flight Mech

*Elsie Diack née Jones*

While at the RAF recruitment centre at Innsworth in December 1942 I was told I could train as a WAAF Teleprinter Operator. However, my eye had been caught by a poster showing a WAAF standing on the wing of an aircraft, smiling and looking down at a handsome young pilot, who was wearing wings and a broad grin. The caption read: *Be a Flight Mechanic and fly with the RAF*. Such was the power of this propaganda that I refused the office job and asked to be a Flight Mechanic…

I passed my technical training course at Hednesford and was posted to RAF Westcott an OTU (Operational Training Unit) of Bomber Command [a station where young RAF crews were being trained to become fully operational], equipped with Wellington bombers. The Flight Mechs, male and female, serviced the aircraft and on completion could be detailed to go up on a test flight. The pilots were very experienced and had usually already done one tour of 'Ops'.

My work consisted of the removal of the brake motor indicator from the pilot's cabin. I would then take it to my section to examine it, clean it and test that it was registering brake pressures correctly. It was then passed by the Flight Engineer and I replaced it on the aircraft. This necessitated lying flat on my back and securing the brake motor with extra safety devices known as split-pins. These were the bane of my existence. They resulted in broken nails, bleeding fingers and a loathing for the plane, the Royal Air Force and the war, in that order!

The large hangars which housed the Wellingtons were open at each end and in mid-winter icy winds blew through, numbing the mind and fingers alike. To protect ourselves we wore a thick vest, sweater, full battledress and over this, heavy drill dungarees, mittens, thick socks, scarves around our ears and a cap on top. We could hardly move when fully dressed and must have presented a weird and wonderful sight as we struggled to get inside the aircraft.

The smell of grease and high-octane fuel sank into our pores and all the perfumes of Araby would not have sweetened the air at our Saturday night village dance, when a cluster of WAAF Flight Mechs grouped together and waited to be asked to dance. But no-one entered our orbit; another reason being that we had plunged our 'best blues' into a small tank of high-octane fuel from which they emerged as new, drying in a few minutes. Although we aired them as long as we could, the smell lingered. Fortunately none of us smoked in those days!

Most evenings I spent in the small NAAFI library where one could escape the noise of our Nissen hut living quarters.

In 1945 when hostilities in Europe ended, airwomen were detailed to be at the airfield to welcome home the POW's, flown back to UK from German POW camps. The men looked tired, unshaven and dirty, and were as shocked at seeing us as we were distressed at seeing them. We took their arms as they emerged from the planes and led them to the de-lousing tent, then to a large hangar where food and hot drinks were served. We were all quiet that night when we came off duty.

War is evil and we can only value the good things like the comradeship, humour and bravery of service personnel and the civilian population. But I was proud to have served as a member of the Women's Auxiliary Air Force.

Working on a Stirling bomber are WAAF trainee fitters on the Fitters Course at Halton 1943. Holding the propeller is Anne Henderson née Benson.

# A Fitter's Tale

*'Doll' Taylor (now Sarah Ann Allen)*

After enlisting in October 1941 I was posted to No. 6 School of Technical Training at RAF Hednesford to become a Flight Mechanic. It was a cold and dreary place in winter. Most girls stuck it out, trying to put together all we had learned about the work, how to keep our hands away from propellers and to not run underneath aircraft – things that used to scare the wits out of us. But we managed to pass out at the end of the course.

In May of the following year six of us were posted to RAF Henlow and were marched to and from work each morning and evening. We worked on Rolls-Royce engines in a hangar. One day we were asked if we would like to go on a course to become Fitters and we decided that we would and so in April 1943 we were sent to No.1 S-of-TT at RAF Halton where we were all lucky enough to pass out with the trade of Fitter II (Engine).

From August to February 1944 we worked on Spitfires, Hurricanes and Lancasters, as well as some French aircraft at 53 OTU Silloth. At Aston Down, working on Hurricanes, we were billeted in Gatcombe House. I was then posted to work on Flying Fortresses at 1674 HCU (Heavy Conversion Unit) RAF Aldergrove, Northern Ireland, where I at last met up with my sister, a Flight Mechanic (Airframe).

The aircraft were located on sites around the tarmac and the work carried out by airwomen on all types of engines depended on the aircraft's flying time and was done at night under arc lamps as well as during the daytime, come rain, shine, snow or ice. Night work was especially cold.

My sister and I worked together, she on airframes and me on engines. Periodic servicing, called 'minors', was more detailed and thorough than ordinary servicing. The Flight Mechs also dealt with petrol refuelling, topping up oil and coolant and making planes ready for take-off.

We each had our own toolboxes, containing a different tool for each different nut, bolt and washer we had to replace and tighten, plus large plug and T spanners. Everything except a hammer – we were not allowed to use brute force! After installing the serviced engine back into the aircraft, we had to time it and check all clearances on inlet and outlet valves, and, as we couldn't start the engines at this time, had to pull the propellers around with our hands until all pistons were correctly positioned ready for a test flight.

We used safety scaffolding on wheels, which we could pull around to enable us to reach the engines. It entailed more in-depth checks, removing most parts of the engine until it was like a skeleton. All components were checked and rechecked before being put back. We stripped engines right down to the crank-shaft, checked pistons for wear and tear, replacing any unserviceable bits. The oil sump was underneath the engine and the oil, the remainder of the fuel in the tanks and the coolant all had to be emptied before taking out the engine. Thick, black, treacle-like oil got into our hair and ran down our arms. In winter the cold and wind did not help our complexions and our faces were very wind-chafed.

Before re-assembling and returning the engine, all parts were thoroughly cleaned and checked and for the crankshaft this was with internal and external micrometers, internally checking piston housing for rough or scored metal and cleaning or renew-ing the starting plugs. We did our work very meticulously in every detail; it was then entered on a Form 700 and signed by the person who had carried out the work.

As I was the Fitter in charge of our aircraft I had to be the one to start the engine. With a bomber aircraft, with help from the pilot, four engines had to be primed beneath and behind the propellers. I had to stand on the wheels in order to carry this out. The slipstream was ferocious, and I had to hang on for dear life until all four were running. Only when the pilot gave the 'thumbs up' sign could I jump down and guide him out to the tarmac.

Spitfires and Hurricanes had Rolls-Royce Merlin engines, which we got to know very well. Special test pilots took the aircraft up on test and sometimes we went with them, but only on the bombers. The Spitfires and Hurricanes had their own test pilots and after they had put these smaller planes through their paces the pilots would do a 'victory roll' to let us know they had passed.

I still keep in touch with many of my friends from that time. We all feel that we were very much in the front line as, without the work and expertise of the ground crews, no aircraft would have left the ground. We feel we were vital to the war effort and worked non-stop to keep the aircraft flying. At the beginning we never dreamed we could accomplish such work and I think we feel all the better for the experience we gained.

# How come?

*Jacqueline Rawlings (ex LAC Jackie Wain)*

We were always last in line at Pay Parades…

…but always first in line for inoculations?

# A Physio in the WAAF

*Betty Dawkins née Dunn*

Betty Dawkins trained as a physiotherapist at the Middlesex Hospital, qualifying in 1940. She joined the WAAF in 1942 after physiotherapists were given acknowledgement as being distinct from nursing orderlies. They were then called 'masseuses'. Promoted to sergeant, Betty was posted to RAF The Leas, a boy's boarding school taken over as a convalescent depot for non-commissioned aircrew. Here she treated a variety of injuries, fractures, burns and others with heat, massage and exercises.

Newspaper pictures of the time showed Betty treating NCOs suffering broken limbs from crashes or shot-up aircraft. One young man's parachute hadn't opened and he was found indented three feet into the ground with horrific injuries yet, several months later, after treatment, he was able to play volleyball at The Leas. It was found that the men injured in combat were the quickest to recover because they were anxious to return to flying for another 'go' at the enemy.

When posted to Rauceby Hospital at Sleaford, Betty treated returning POW's suffering with beriberi and other ailments.

From her posting to the RAF Physical Medical Centre in London, she still has photographs of the visit made there by Her Majesty Queen Mary. Her final posting was to the hospital at RAF Cosford.

# A Dicey Drive

*Betty Chapple née Connolly*

In the spring of 1944, after training as a Wireless Operator, I was posted to HQ No.1 Group, Bomber Command, Bawtry Hall. Here we had a tight schedule and after a few months my health suffered because I couldn't sleep during the day, so I was posted to Hemswell for day work only.

On the day I was posted, five airmen were also in the van to be posted at various other stations in the Group. A WAAF driver and an MT Officer made eight people in the van and we were packed in with kit bags and luggage wedged between our knees and feet. I was to be dropped off first so, as we approached Hemswell, our driver cut over the airfield and straight across the runway, unaware that a Lancaster was about to land. As she saw it she screamed and stopped the van in the middle of the runway, and every person in the van was deafened with the roar of the four engines at full throttle going over our heads. As we recovered from the shock, as you can imagine, the Officer shouted some very ungentlemanly words to the driver!

Next day, while I was working in Flying Control, an irate pilot came to ask, "Who was that dumb clot who parked a van in the middle of the runway as I was landing yesterday? I had a hell of a job to overshoot". I was pleased to see the man whose skill had saved us and his crew, but thought it better to keep quiet about being a passenger in the van...

I enjoyed my service days and made many friends.

# Fond Memories of Orkney

*Sibell Clay*

In April 1942 almost the entire WAAF contingent at RAF Canewdon in Essex were posted and given seven days leave, but not told where we were going. After leave we all met at Euston station to board the night train to Inverness. We were a mixture of trades: Radar/Ops, Tele/Ops, Admin clerks, Cooks, GDs and Medical orderlies. The officer in charge was Section Officer C.A.M. England.

After transport to Bunchrew House, HQ No.70 Signals Wing, we were on our way to the Orkney Islands by train from Inverness to the transit camp at Thurso, a short journey to Scrabster and embarkation on the *Earl of Zetland*. Four hours later we disembarked at Stromness. From our RAF transport, our first sight of the Radar Unit at Netherbutton was of eight majestic pylons standing on top of a hill overlooking Scapa Flow, which was busy with ships of the Royal Navy. We were the first unit of WAAF to arrive on the Orkneys.

Apart from Radar Mechanics, some Cooks and GDs, the men had been posted away. Those who remained gave us a warm welcome. They had organised the boiler which served our quarters, so we had loads of hot water to greet us.

Netherbutton was to become the happiest of stations and a lovely relationship was soon established with the local people. They were wonderful.

The Radar Ops, Radar Mechs and Tele Ops worked a four watch system: 0800-1300 hours, 13.00-1800 hrs, 1800-midnight and midnight-0800 hrs. After night duty the rule was bed for the morning and the rest of the day was free. Most evenings we were allowed out until 2200hrs, with two late passes weekly, signing out and in at the Guard Room.

Four months later tragedy struck. On 23rd August the Commer vehicle transporting WAAF girls to visit another station was involved in an accident on the Deerness Road, killing two Radar Ops (Sheila Munro, aged 19 and Gill Marr, aged 20) and injuring four others. Being a very close, small unit, the shock stayed with us for a long time.

Social activities were in abundance – both our own dances and invitations to other camps, including the Army and Royal Navy. Many ENSA shows visited Orkney and some of the stars who appeared became post-war celebrities. Local service talent was also very good, with one show, 'Wings Over Orkney', being cast from Netherbutton and Bignold Park, the costumes for a dance routine made from barrage balloon fabric and the bomb blast material as used on the windows of public transport!

On Sundays a board would appear outside our NAAFI reading 'RAFIES bring your WAAFIES to the NAAFI CAFIES'.

Apart from these social events, we had many invitations and hospitality shown to us by the local people. Other popular invitations were from the personnel on destroyers and battleships of the fleet anchored in Scapa Flow, a drifter being sent to collect and take us to the ship. Climbing the rope ladder onto the deck of the huge battleship *King George V* was precarious, especially if a good old Orkney gale was in progress. After being shown around we were treated to a gorgeous meal with food we had not seen since pre-war days, coming away with our coat pockets stuffed with goodies that only the Royal Navy could supply. The extra weight made climbing down the rope ladder even more precarious. Another bonus of being based on Orkney was that we were able to send butter and eggs to our families at home.

Our term of duty was six months, extended to nine months but, lucky me, I remained there for twenty-two months.

Midnight communion at Christmas 1943 was celebrated in the NAAFI by Rev. A.R. Johnston, the RAF Chaplain. The weather was very cold with some snow. On Christmas morning Pip Matthews decided that all in our hut should get up at 0600 hours, dress in sweaters and slacks, go over to the men's billets and tip them out of bed! I think we played hockey in the afternoon after a good lunch served to us by the officers. The day ended with an all ranks dance in the NAAFI attended by all except those on duty. My memories of my two Christmases on Orkney will never be forgotten. I quote the words recently spoken to me by an Air Force friend:

*"Out of the bloodiest of wars I met and made friends with some wonderful and truly remarkable people..."*

For me that includes the people of Orkney, who referred to us as 'the girls at the pylons'.

---

### Dem bones, dem bones. Dem dry bones...
### Recycling 1940s-style

Two ordinary ounces of bones will make sufficient cordite to fire two shots from a Hurricane's guns, feed one hen for half a day, provide glue to stick one shell container or enough fertiliser to produce 4lbs of potatoes. Bones also made the glue used in the distemper which was painted into the zebra markings used on aircraft for D-Day.

# Work at Station Sick Quarters

*Mary Ross Roberts née Sinclair*

My initiation into the ways of Air Force life began in October 1941 at Bridgnorth and after a month at Pannal Ash, Harrogate, I was posted to the RAF Hospital at Yatesbury, then on to SSQ at RAF Hemswell, a Bomber Command station in Lincolnshire. Both English and Polish Squadrons were based there.

At Sick Quarters I met Jessie Barlow and we have remained close friends, meeting up from time to time. Jessie's husband was an MT driver at Hemswell and sometimes did ambulance duty with us.

My stay there was a happy one, considering our duties and the times we lived in. We worked hard, looking after the needs of both male and female patients. We were in close contact with the bomber aircrews who flew practically every night. When on 'drome duty' with the ambulance we had to issue each pilot with a box of 'wakey-wakey' (amphetamine) tablets to keep the crew awake on their return journey. We sat in the ambulance under the control tower until all take-offs were completed, then returned to the same spot hours later to count them back in again. Of course, some did not return, either shot down or diverted to other stations because of damage. This was one of the worst aspects, for we had come to know both English and Polish crews well and had become good comrades.

Some airmen came back badly shot up and were taken straight to SSQ for treatment and sometimes transferred to the hospital in Lincoln. We became used to traumatic incidents, worked well together and helped each other over the worst of them. It grieves me that SSQ staff have received only minimal mention in other accounts of those dreadful days; great work was done and many lives were saved by those unsung heroes and heroines.

When the tide of war turned and events became easier I went on many training courses, one of which was an Air Ambulance course at Hendon, which resulted in my eventually flying with wounded personnel – often a very sad and heart-breaking task, but again, some lives were saved.

Having had experience of working alongside Polish aircrew and acquiring something of their language, I was posted to Flying Training Command at Penrhos, Pwllheli in North Wales. I worked there with some very good doctors, some Polish, as were others of the staff, and this increased my knowledge of their language and I made many friends.

Two years ago I returned to Hemswell and the visit renewed many memories of lads and lassies I had been able to help years before, and somehow gave me a little peace of mind. The same thing occurred on a visit to Penrhos, which is now a resettlement camp for some of the Polish aged.

My time with the RAF ended in May 1946 and for the most part I enjoyed my nearly five years' service and made many friends, having treated just about every rank from AC Plonk to Air Commodore, NAAFI girls and wives of RAF personnel.

# A Waaf at Bletchley Park

*Audrey Webster née Pye*

Much publicity has been given to the codebreakers of Bletchley Park, but little has been said about the many other men and women who worked there. I was one of many WAAF, a Wireless Op/Morse Slip Reader (or in Naval terms, a High Speed Telegraphist). We were vetted before being allowed in and issued with a pass, which had to be shown whenever we entered the Park; no pass, no entry, even though we may have been well known to the guards. In our section, which contained very noisy equipment, we had circuits to places like Alexandria, Colombo, Delhi, Taranto, Bari and other places, and worked an 8 hour, 4 watch system, two days on each watch; 4pm-to-midnight, midnight-to-8am, 8am-to-4pm, then 48 hours clear. Apart from the high-speed equipment we had hand circuits to various places, and after D-Day one opened to France. Despite the fact that all messages were in code it was most interesting and we who worked it felt very much in touch with events.

There was a great feeling of comradeship between operators at either end of the wires on both the high-speed and the hand circuits. The secrecy was kept for years after the war ended, greatly to the credit of all who worked there. Secrecy became something of a habit; there was no fraternisation between trades and to this day I doubt if any were knowledgeable about all the workings of the Park, but we all felt, even if we were only a small cog in a huge machine, that we were making a valuable contribution towards victory.

Church Green, Bletchley. Right, front is Audrey Webster.

# Too Much Information

*Peggy Rowell née Brennan*

My first posting after passing out from RAF Cranwell with the grand sounding title of RTO/VHF/DF Operator was to RAF Manston, a forward relay from RAF Hornchurch. I was in the Transmitter Block and had to operate a switch when told to 'transmit' by the controller at Hornchurch.

Equipped with log book and pen, I then had to log everything that passed between the controller and pilots in the air.

I had been instructed on my course to log every word; it was important, I was told, and I must not miss *anything*. I duly did as I was told, but was surprised at the rather forthright language used by the pilots when communicating with each other…

At the end of my first day the Signals Officer (who vetted the log each day) sent for me.

"I want to congratulate you on your immaculate logging," he said, "very clear and, I am sure, accurate. However, there is no need to write down anything other than the conversation between controller and pilot. The interchanges between pilots in combat do not need to be logged. I am impressed but surprised that one of your tender years (I was 18) even *knows* some of these words, never mind knowing how to spell them!"

I was not sure whether I had been complimented or ticked off!

# The First Night of the Blitz

*Wynne Morgan*

When I joined the WAAF I was posted to No. 1 Balloon Centre, Kidbrook in South East London. I was highly delighted because I lived in Bow and so could get home on 24-hour passes.

One Saturday my friend Audrey was going home with me, and I had sweet-talked a shopkeeper into selling me a box of my Mum's favourite 'Black Magic' chocolates. Waiting for a bus to take us through the Blackwall Tunnel we saw a dogfight going on up above us. Young and exuberant we cheered our boys on, little knowing what a horrifying experience lay in front of us. I was looking forward to seeing Mum, Dad and younger brother Derek, but before we entered the tunnel, an air-raid siren sounded and we had to get off the bus and go into a shelter, like an underground cavern – dirty, smelly and damp. Many people were there, including small, crying children. After half an hour I started handing round Mum's chocolates.

I stood at the shelter door for a crafty smoke and saw that everywhere was bright red. I thought, 'Oh God I'm dead and gone to hell!' Fire engine bells were ringing, there were bangs and more bangs. I thought, 'there is no way I will ever see my beloved family again.' At about five in the morning the all-clear siren went and we got a lift in a ten-tonner through the tunnel, but that was as far as we could go. We just stood there with burning rubble all around; smoke, debris, pools of water. The East India Docks were completely gone. AFS and air raid wardens were everywhere and told us we could only get to Bow, four miles away, by 'Shanks's Pony'.

Dirty and tired, we walked through the bombed-out East India Dock Road; the most heartbreaking sight I had ever seen.

Finally we got to the corner of my street. The corner shop had gone. I turned my back and said to Audrey,

"I can't look. Tell me what you see."

"The left hand side of the road has gone," she answered, "on the right are a crowd of people at a gate, laughing, crying and cuddling one another." I turned around, tears streaming, and a shout went up.

"She's here! There's my Wynne!" Then Mum, Dad, Derek, aunts, uncles and my little Gran, all came running down the street, arms outstretched.

We were all together for a few brief hours. Dad had hung a huge Union Jack from the top of the house. There wasn't a window or door intact, but Derek, with typical cockney humour had chalked 'Window Cleaner Wanted'.

Our shoe soles had bubbled through walking over burning pavements. Dad repaired them before we returned to camp.

That was just the first night of the Blitz, to be followed by many similar nights, but it is a night I will never forget.

# Blown Out of Bed

*Flight Sergeant May Hancock (now Lall)*

Busy at our desks in the Record Office at Ruislip on a sunny afternoon in August 1940, we heard the roar of an aircraft engine. There was no warning, but taking no chances we went straight down on the floor under our desks. A German fighter thundered over the street outside, machine-gunning all windows at the front of our office. The whole thing was over in seconds.

Going back to our billets later, we saw the High Street with every shop window shattered and goods spilled out into the street.

That evening 'Jerry' came back with his bombers. Bombs dropped into a nearby pond and blew me out of bed, mattress and all, into what seemed like a dark hole.

It was pitch dark, but luckily for me a passing mobile ack-ack battery blew the blackout off the window and I saw that I had been flung into my cupboard!

When the guns became silent, I crept back to bed, ending one of the most eventful days of my life.

# A Pigeon Keeper's Tale

*Kathleen Busby, née Coysh*

When I became a Pigeon Keeper in the WAAF, a duty I held for six months, being part of the responsibility of the signals section, I thought it would be an easy job, but there was much more to it than I at first thought…

My posting was to Thorney Island, Hampshire, a wartime station of Coastal Command, whose job it was to seek out and destroy enemy shipping in the English Channel. My team consisted of two airmen, three airwomen, a WAAF driver and one truck to transport pigeons from the loft to the waiting aircraft.

It was our duty to maintain and supply suitable pigeons for use by the aircrews when they were sent on missions, as this was a form of contact with their base in the event of being brought down into the sea.

We raised many birds in our loft and could draw on other birds from civilian pigeon-keepers who had been registered with the Air Ministry. When we raised our own stock they were ringed at one week old and entered into the log book. The fitness and training of these birds was entirely our responsibility. As a point of interest, a fully grown pigeon should weigh between 14 and 16 ounces. They become trainable at 10-12 weeks old and can then begin their training programme.

First our birds were taken within a 20-mile radius of their home loft and released, and this was done many times to make sure they returned each time. Only when they were declared 'fit for active service' were they put on aircraft.

Records had to be kept up to date regarding the number of birds ready and available for service at any given time. Before they were sent on operational flights the following details had to be noted:

- a metal tag on the bird's leg which held the SOS white strip;
- the colour code of the station;
- the colour code of the RAF, which was always blue (other branches of the armed forces also used pigeons, so each had their own colour code).

Flight crews were issued with an indelible pencil to be used to write on the white strip to tell us of their known position if they were brought down. They were given lectures on how to handle the pigeons, as it was imperative that they became fully aware of the important part these birds might play in their survival in case of a forced landing. In the event of such a message being received at base it would have to be delivered with all haste to the signals officer, who would call out the air/sea rescue service – vital in saving airmen's lives. It was not unknown for enemy shipping to pick up our stranded aircrew before we got to them, so speed was of the essence in the rescue.

When the birds returned to the loft after a mission they were examined for stress or injury and if found to be unfit they were put into sick bay, where they stayed until fully recovered, so you see they were as well cared for as any other personnel!

Birds in the service of the RAF had to have their rings marked: *'RAF MPS-Report to Signals, Air Ministry, London'* – in case lost birds were found by someone other than service personnel. The Air Ministry had to be informed as soon as possible.

I well remember on one occasion being called upon to supply birds for an operational flight to take off at dawn. Unfortunately our driver overslept and when we arrived at the waiting aircraft I was greeted with a gruff, 'You're late!' from a very angry pilot.

That didn't happen again!

Pigeons in their hundreds served during the war, but only one was featured by the Imperial War Museum. This was Winkie, an RAF pigeon serving in a Beaufort which ditched in the North Sea in February 1942. Despite being covered in oil, she flew 120 miles home, enabling the crew to be rescued. She was awarded The Dickin medal (the animal's VC) for bravery and attended a celebration dinner with the crew she helped to save.

# The 'Pigeon Farm' at RAF Waddington

It must have been a farm cottage originally and was whitewashed and, if memory serves me, thatched. In this the corporal pigeon keeper cared for his charges in large cages. The cottage was tiny but there was ample room for the pigeons. Here the smaller cages for the birds going 'on ops' were filled each night. I don't know if all those released got back home, but at least those in returning aircraft did. I went one day to have a look around and was allowed to hold and stroke one of the pigeons while the corporal explained to me how things were done.

When visiting Waddington in later years I looked for the pigeon cottage, but it was gone. It had seemed so incongruous standing there between the hangars and other airfield buildings, so very rural and rather touching.

---

The humble pigeon could be very important in the dark days of war. There was a story of an Australian Army pigeon keeper in WWI who, tiring of sending messages by pigeon carrier from the trenches, put forward the suggestion that pigeons should be crossed with cockatoos and taught to speak…

---

# An MT Mechanic's Tale

*Sue Denison née Link, Canada*

I joined the WAAF a few months before I was 18. Soon I was off to Innsworth to begin basic training. At first it was scary, not knowing anyone and not having been away from home before. Some girls cried and wanted to go home, but the rest of us stuck it out and soon knew what joining up was all about. After collecting gear, bedding and inoculations, the fun began; route marches, drills, gas drill and many other things. Oh those blistered feet! But we toughened up after a few days and formed a proud squad. At the end of recruit training we were informed that Motor Transport Mechanics and Flight Mechanics were needed, so I and Ella, with whom I had made friends, decided to be MTMs. Within a day or so we were on our way to Weeton, near Blackpool, where we met a new set of girls, who were great. With their comradeship we became like one big family.

We had a lot to learn at classes. The first morning in shop we didn't know what to expect. We were all given benches and toolboxes and a piece of metal which we were to make a square out of. Signs on the bench read DON'T LEAVE TOOLBOXES IN THE AISLE. When I pulled my toolbox out I became so engrossed in my work that I forgot and a little later the Sergeant came marching down the aisle reading orders, and suddenly, thump, he was on the floor.

The room went silent and his face was as red as mine as he got up, saying a few blankety-blank words. Then a girl said, "I wish the sergeant had fallen for me on my first day in shop" and everyone laughed, even the sergeant.

But I never left my toolbox out again...

It was a hard course, with a lot of drawing of parts of the engine, how to clean spark plugs, reseat valves, etc, and learn the firing numbers of the engines. Plus oil and grease all the vehicles. The course lasted four and a half months. After it was finished we were sent home on ten days leave, and I was ready to go.

From home I was posted to RAF Credenhill near Hereford, a gorgeous city on the River Wye, and quite a journey from home. The first morning I was up early, did all my chores in the hut, got my dungarees and boots on and set out for the MT Section and reported in. This place, after the training course, where we used a lot of pressure tools, was somewhat different. A small Fordson car sat over the pit, and as I walked in a very tall corporal handed an object to me and told me to do a 500 mile inspection on the Fordson. I kept looking at the object he had given me and he asked me what was wrong.

"What is it?" I asked.

"A grease gun," he said. "Now get to work!"

The corporal and I were the only mechanics. Being a small unit there weren't many trucks, two ambulances and two coal trucks. When the WAAF drivers drove the coal trucks we always got a little extra for our billets. One duty night we heard a plane coming down and looking out saw a Flying Fortress crash on the other side of the road. We got the WAAF drivers out with the ambulances and off they went. Unfortunately, the aircraft was a blazing inferno, we could hear screams, but the eight airmen could not be saved. It was a dreadful time.

On D-Day we were all confined to camp. In the afternoon I received a telegram from my mother asking me to go home as soon as possible. As I had beaten our WAAF Officer in the 100 yards race in sports the day before, she said she hoped I hadn't come asking for favours. No-one was supposed to have passes that day, but after I told her my mother needed me she said she could give me 36 hours beginning from noon next day. So I stayed that night in Hereford at a hostel, and during the night I was pulled out of bed by the Military Police and asked for my pass. They wanted to take me back to camp, but after a few telepone calls, they let me stay.

Sue with Yatesbury ambulance

On returning to Credenhill I was granted a compassionate posting to Yatesbury, which meant I could go home more often. Yatesbury was a larger station, and the MT section had a ramp which held four or five vehicles, and it was back to pressure tools again. There was a large ambulance column and I was assigned to work on twelve of them with a corporal. He was very nice and we got along well. Because the ambulances were on the road continually, they needed more attention. I made 500 mile, 1,000 mile inspections, and 10,000 miles was a complete strip down of the engines, plugs sand blasted and reset, valves ground by hand, and we had to be sure the seating was perfect. All parts were washed in gasoline, so we really smelt at the end of the day with grease all over us. There was much more work here and we had three WAAF mechanics. The oldest one we called 'Mother' and we took all our problems to her. She would wake us up in the night to go for hot showers or to do our washing while the water was hot.

MT Mechanics at work (Names not known) Courtesy RAF Museum, Hendon
Ref: PC1998/164/140

One day I was under the ramp working on a truck when I heard a deep voice say, "Come out from under there honey, don't you hide". I looked out and saw a black American soldier staring down at me. He'd come in to refuel, as they so often did.

Our WAAF ambulance drivers had to make many trips to Southampton to pick up wounded men and take them to hospitals all over the country. Sometimes I went with them. I think of those girls driving ambulances with canvas doors, no windshield wipers, no heating, and the wind whistling right through. I am so proud of all the WAAF who took part during the War, no matter what they did, and I get cross when I hear men say that women can't do this or that when we did so many things all those years ago. I will never forget the comradeships and friendships that we still have today.

# The 'Glamorous' Life of the WAAF

*Bert Wilkinson*

"We now take you over to the Palm Court ballroom
for dancing until midnight…"

# Missing

*by Herbert Corby*

They told me, when they cut the ready wheat
The hares are suddenly homeless and afraid
And aimlessly circle the stubble with scared feet
Finding no home in sunlight or in shade

It's morning and the Hampdens have returned;
The crews are home, have stretched and laughed and gone.
Whence the planes came and the bright neon burned,
The sun has ridden the sky and made the dawn.

He walks distraught, circling the landing ground,
Waiting. The last one in that won't come back.
And like those hares he wanders round and round,
Bereft and desolate on the close-cropped track.

# The Balloon Girls

*Beryl Williams*

One of the more physically demanding trades that WAAF air-women undertook was that of Balloon Operator. When the RAF first decided to replace servicemen with girls in order to release the men for other duties, it was assumed that twenty girls were needed to replace a male crew of nine, but gradually this number was reduced, and eventually a WAAF crew numbered twelve.

Their training included the splicing of wire ropes, hard on hands unused to such work, how to operate a winch, and learning the names of different parts that made up a balloon. Flying was a strenuous task, involving a girl on the winch, protected from flying steel cables by a metal guard, and others around the balloon releasing the wire ropes which fastened it down on 120lb concrete blocks and lifting 40lb sandbags at each operation.

The inner and outer rings of barrage balloons flying over cities forced enemy aircraft to fly above them, whereby they could be attacked by our fighter planes and anti aircraft guns.

Sites were usually well away from RAF stations, which meant the girls had no access to a NAAFI or station entertainments such as dances, cinemas or concerts. They had to prepare and cook their own meals and the quality of these depended on the skill of that day's duty cook. Another duty, surely an eerie and lonely one, was that of sentry patrol, when two girls armed with nothing more than truncheons and whistles against possible intruders kept vigil while the rest of the crew were sleeping.

Barrage balloons were not identical; they came in different sizes according to where they were to be flown, some of them from ships and some with armaments attached to the central steel cable.

# Memories of a Balloon Operator

*Olga Twist*

Olga Twist, who served as a balloon operator at various locations in the UK, has the following reminiscences…

Barrage balloons were always hard work to storm bed down. On one very bad, stormy night, the balloon on the dock site at Avonmouth, manned by a male crew, broke loose and both balloon and winch ended up in the water; the winch-man having jumped clear just in time.

While serving at Shirehampton we would sometimes receive the order 'Albino Release' with a height given, which meant we had to fly a medium-sized, cream-coloured balloon with a small bomb attached, then release it at the height given, rock it, and it would explode. Our site never had an accident with this.

At a site in Birmingham two young men attacked the girls on guard duty and in going out to help I was knocked down and one of the men started to choke me. Eventually the police arrived and the men were arrested. At the trial the judge only reprimanded the lads because they were in the Merchant Navy and were serving on the Russian Convoys. *The Daily Mirror* reported the case and asked why WAAF personnel were expected to stand guard armed with just a baton, while airmen performing the same role had a rifle… but nothing changed.

Balloon crew at work. Kneeling 2nd left is Myra Heaps, Abbottsford B.C.

Balloon Operators on Wings for Victory parade in Sheffield, August 1941.
Front rank, 2nd from right is Myra Heaps.

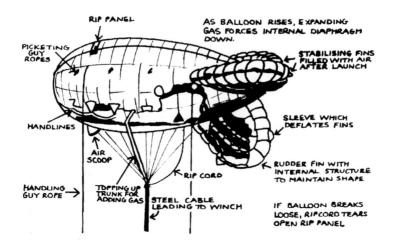

RIP PANEL

AS BALLOON RISES, EXPANDING
GAS FORCES INTERNAL DIAPHRAGM
DOWN.

PICKETING
GUY
ROPES

STABILISING FINS
FILLED WITH AIR
AFTER LAUNCH

HANDLINES

SLEEVE WHICH
DEFLATES FINS

AIR
SCOOP

RUDDER FIN WITH
INTERNAL STRUCTURE
TO MAINTAIN SHAPE

RIP CORD

HANDLING
GUY ROPE

TOPPING UP
TRUNK FOR
ADDING GAS

STEEL CABLE
LEADING TO WINCH

IF BALLOON BREAKS
LOOSE, RIPCORD TEARS
OPEN RIP PANEL

## ANATOMY OF A BARRAGE BALLOON

| | |
|---|---|
| Length | 66ft |
| Diameter | 18ft |
| Height | 30ft |
| Material | 600 separate pieces of Egyptian cotton, assembled on opposite bias and totalling 1000 sq. yds. material. |
| Cost | £500 |
| Coating | "Dope" – a black rubber, waterproof undercoat, and an aluminium varnish top coat. |
| Gas | 20,000 cu. ft. hydrogen per balloon; 60 cylinders required per launch; cost £50 per launch. |

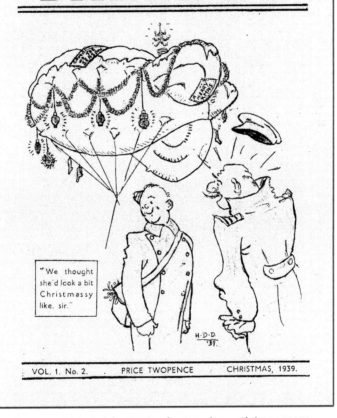

The second issue of the RAF Bowlee Newsletter, Christmas 1939

# Dusk Take-Off, 1940

*by Ronald Ransom*

At the end of the runway
The WAAF corporal lingers
Nervously threading
A scarf through her fingers,

Husband? Or lover?
Or friend for a night?
Her face doesn't tell
In the dim evening light.

The Squadron is airborne
But still the WAAF lingers
Nervously threading
A scarf through her fingers.

# On Yer Bike

*Veronica Butcher née Bennett, Canada*

I joined the WAAF in 1943, and after finishing a Flight/Mech course at Rugeley in Staffordshire, I was posted to Hampstead Norris, a satellite of No.15 OTU, Harwell. A few months later we learned that the station was to close and we were all going to be sent temporarily to Harwell. D-Day was approaching and Harwell was to be handed over, with our satellite, to the American Air Force – so we later learned.

When the day for our departure arrived we were told to assemble at the guard room at 08.00 hours with our kit and bicycles. There were more than one hundred of us, all various ranks and trades. Our kitbags were loaded onto trucks and the order given us to 'mount and start pedalling'. NCOs raced back and forth trying to keep everyone together but they had a hopeless task. Some bikes had punctures, and of course no spares, while other riders couldn't keep up. I was one of these, my little legs couldn't pedal fast enough. I had my own bicycle, which was smaller than the others, me being a short person. Some show offs, with their smart bikes, ended up in the ditch. It was well past dinner-time before I and other stragglers finally made it to Harwell, hungry and exhausted. The twenty-mile ride had seemed more like fifty!

I was born in London, but as I was only 17 and a half when I enlisted, I took my Dad's nationality and had permission to wear the CANADA flash on my tunic. Dad was also in the RAF, a Flying Control Officer. During the Dambusters raid, he was stationed at Scampton with 617 Squadron and knew the crew well.

In November 1945 Dad took Mother and me to Canada, but I returned to UK and rejoined the WAAF as a Drill Instructor, stationed at Wilmslow from 1947-1949.

On their station bikes are Veronica Butcher, Frances Marr, Kathleen O'Hara and Georgie Geddes.

The following two stories, which appeared in WAAF Association News recall a tragic night when a German V1 rocket struck a block of flats in Kensington where hundreds of WAAFs were billeted...

## I Was Hit by a Doodle-Bug...

*N.K. Ashby, née Flowers*

I was in Hut 146 at Bletchley Park, but before this I was at South Kensington, billeted in Thursley Court, a tall block of flats. I was sleeping on the third floor when a doodle-bug hit the building.

I was injured and was taken to Brompton Hospital, and then next day to Ashford Hospital. By the time I recovered and returned to the course I was on at Compton Bassett, I could not find out what had happened to my friends. Does anyone remember just what happened that night?

## So Was I...

*Pamela J. Anderson, USA*

I remember all the events before the bomb hit us. We used to get up every night and sit in the corridors with our gas masks and helmets, then as soon as the 'all clear' was given we would go up to our room and no sooner get back in bed before the air raid warning would go again. This was very tiring as we got no sleep so, finally, we were allowed to stay in bed during the air raids.

The raids got much worse and we had doodle-bugs dropping all around us. We requested some short of shelter. The Air Force had a shelter across the road. The Commanding Officer was very annoyed with us, saying she could put us on a court martial for complaining in a group. She came up with the idea of evacuating the top two floors and the rest could stay in bed.

The following night we were hit –168 girls were injured and 8 were killed. I escaped injury and was able to find stairs and climb down. Firemen and GIs rescued us.

It was so dark after the bomb hit; I had a small chair beside my bed that was blown to pieces along with my flashlight. We were taken to a shelter wearing just our pyjamas and stayed that way for about three days.

I was sent home for a while and then on to Compton Bassett for a course and then to Hut 8 at Bletchley Park.

# Tragedy in the Fog

*Florence Philips*

I served as a Radio Operator at Hack Green, an operational Ground Control Interception station, from January 1943 to May 1944, but much time was spent in training aircrew (who had been taken off flying for a break) as Controllers.

There were eight airwomen in a Radar crew with a Corporal in charge of each watch. We worked in the Ops room, my position being the 'height tube'. This involved comparing the ratio between two blips which appeared on the tube for a split second as the aerial tracked the aircraft. When the blips faded, the position of the aircraft could be calculated.

Hack Green consisted of wooden huts, our only neighbours being Frank Furber, the farmer, and Patty, the railway level-crossing keeper. We had to leave our friendly private billets and move into a hotel when Hack Green was extended to take in the army ack-ack battery, but the friendship of the local people came to the fore when disaster struck my crew after we had been on duty one foggy night in December 1943.

I decided to get in the first transport back to our billet available – the 'Old Coach' – rather than wait for the rest of the watch, who travelled behind in the 'Horse-Box'. Patty had now retired, and the new crossing keeper waved us across…

In horror I saw the railway engine's lamp almost upon the gates as we crossed the line, but the Horse Box close behind us was caught broadside and carried up the line, smashed to matchwood.

We helped the injured and Frank Furber set up a first aid station at his farm. There were two dead and fourteen injured. Cpl Doxon's hand was severely maimed, and all I could do for him was bandage it with a handkerchief. Ambulances from Crewe took the casualties to Wilmslow Hospital and the following Sunday a memorial service was held in Nantwich church.

I was posted to South Devon just before D-Day. The invasion fleet was massing in all the inlets along the coast. A cargo ship carrying Sunlight soap and tinned sausages was torpedoed in the Channel. After Customs clearance we were allowed to collect the soap to send home, provided we did not give our address. Some families had enough soap to last them until the end of the war and rationing.

Then I was posted to Flamborough, where I helped operate a mobile GCI station on the top of the cliffs, the object being to try to prevent enemy bombers destroying runways before our Lancasters could return from bombing raids.

# 'Admin' wasn't all Drill and Discipline

...........................................................................

*Beryl Williams née Stockwell*

Living in London during the Battle of Britain was an extraordinary time and watching the dogfights going on overhead was an amazing sight. We cheered when we saw an enemy aircraft downed, not thinking of the consequence for any person on the ground when it crashed. The Battle of Britain pilots were our heroes and photos of them in the newspapers showed handsome young men smiling and waving as though life was wonderful for them. At night we sought refuge in various types of shelters and jumped at the sound of the ack-ack guns mounted on lorries parked in streets, hoping the dropping bombs didn't 'have our names on them'. Once a week I stayed at the company I worked for at Lincoln's Inn Fields for my fire-watching shift and some nights were very busy and noisy.

The recruiting poster for the WAAF with its invitation to 'Join the WAAF and Serve with the Men Who Fly' was a powerful message and enticed many of us to enlist and get to meet and work with the heroes of the RAF. It certainly enticed me, although I came from a regular army family, and having been brought up in army married quarters in the UK and Egypt, should really have joined the ATS. My retired father, an ex-Warrant Officer, had rejoined the army and was commissioned into the RASC, but was pleased to have another family member in uniform; later my younger sister also enlisted in the WAAF.

My first attempt to enlist, at Kingsway in 1940, was foiled by a WAAF Officer who detected my lie when I said I was 18 years old (I was 17 yrs 9 months) and asked me to come back with my birth certificate. Only a few months later the age limit was dropped to 17 and a half. By that time I was already in the

WAAF, having enlisted at the Bristol WAAF recruiting centre while staying with my mother's sister in Calne.

I was sent with five other girls for training at Innsworth. I had wanted to become an MT Driver but was turned down because I did not have a licence already – at that time I believe the RAF was not training girls as drivers, although later they did. After confessing that I had been working as a shorthand typist I was given the trade of Clerk/General Duties.

I took recruit training at Innsworth in my stride and even the injections, route marches and lectures didn't put me off (though the slides they showed us about the diseases we would catch if we didn't 'behave ourselves' horrified me – so innocent, most of us were!). I failed to understand some of the homesick girls who cried in their beds at night. I was not to have any trade training; after the course my first posting was to the Recruiting Centre at Kingsway – the very place that had turned me down! It seems it had been decided at the start that I would make a Recruiter…

My father was living at home on his own, being stationed at Regents Park, so I was billeted at my own home. My mother was in Calne with my Aunt, as her health had suffered in the raids. One sister was in the National Fire Service whereas the eldest, with her baby along with my younger brother had been separately evacuated to Wales and my younger sister was with my mother. This interlude lasted for just one week, and then I was returned to Bristol to work at the Combined Recruiting Centre in Prewett Street, near Temple Meads railway station, to endure a few more air raids, after being told that the former airwomen staff had been injured and pulled from the rubble of their bombed out billet!

We were billeted at the YWCA in Pembroke Road, ruled over and taken good care of by Miss Overman. When I told her I had a boyfriend – a regular airman I'd met in Calne – but that my parents thought I was too young to be engaged, she told me she had wanted, but was forbidden by her parents, to be engaged at 16 years old before her young man had left for the trenches in World War I, where he was killed. She was very emotional when she told me of this, her memory of him still sharp. She had never married. "One is never too young to fall in love," she said.

Rae, 'Tibs' and Beryl, RAF Recruiting Office Bristol 1941.

With three other girls, Muriel, 'Tibs' and Rae, I worked on documentation for the stream of fresh-faced young men, or boys as most of them were, who came to the centre from a wide area around the city, from villages in Somerset, Gloucester and Wiltshire to enlist in the RAF. They were very respectful to us girls, who were already serving and wearing Air Force Blue uniforms.

We took all their details, filled the documents in triplicate, I think, gave each a service number with instructions to commit it to memory and took them into the CO, a Flight Lieutenant, to be inducted and take the oath. We then sent them home to await posting instructions and a railway warrant.

Years later I met one of the boys again. I was walking along near Trafalgar Square on my way to meet my husband (we had married in 1942) when a shout of 'Corporal!' stopped me. Not recognising the young man who had called to me, I walked on, but he ran across and said, "You gave me my number in Bristol and I told you I would be aircrew..."

I noticed he wore a white aircrew training flash in his cap.

"Don't you remember me?"

"Of course," I said, not recognising him from Adam.

We stood and chatted for a while and then shook hands and parted. I do hope he survived the war. I often wonder what happened to all those bright, eager boys and like to think that they all survived to live peacefully with their families somewhere in the West Country, although the sad fact is that, statistically, only about half of them would have done so.

After a year I became restless and wanted to be in the 'proper' air force, on an active station but my requests for a posting were turned down, so I remustered and this was granted. I still couldn't be a driver, as we could not remuster 'down' (trades were sorted into groups numbered 1 to 5 and each had a different pay structure) so I plumped for the fairly new trade of 'Administrative'. Eventually this came through and I returned to Innsworth for a two-week course, ending as a corporal with a posting to Station X. I went back to Bristol to pack up and tried to find out where Station X was. Nobody had ever heard of it, but a railway warrant for Bletchley was sent to me, so I knew it must be around there somewhere.

At Bletchley station I looked around, wondering where to go, remembering the cartoons in the train carriages, of Hitler and Co, with large ears, hiding under railway compartment and restaurant seats to overhear secrets, and the posters exhorted service people to 'keep mum' about their work and movements, but a porter approached me and asked if I wanted 'Bletchley Park'. Hopefully I said 'Yes'. He gave me directions and I soon walked there without any problem.

All of us at Station X, whether RAF, Army, Navy or Foreign Office staff, had to be positively vetted before being given a pass and from then on we had to show our pass every time we went in the gate.

At first I worked in the WAAF Orderly Room on billeting duties, trying to match up girls with landladies, to avoid possible problems, and during our lunch break I and another couple of girls were taught to use a .303 rifle by a bemused, elderly Army officer, as we stretched out on the grassy bank, aiming at the Mansion. Of course the rifles were not loaded, so we were no threat to anyone, not even to the enemy.

I then took charge of Shenley Park, home of Lady Cadman, who lived in one of the wings, and used as a hostel for, mostly, Wireless Ops and Teleprinter Ops working shift duties in the huts at Station X on sensitive work. They were daily bussed into camp and back again and there were always some of them sleeping during the daytime when they worked on late shifts at night.

There was a small permanent staff, Corporal Samuel was i/c the cookhouse, and produced good meals for us and, whenever I could arrange a party or dance for the girls there and ask in a few RAF boys from Chicksands, came up with snacks for them. My job was to run the hostel, keep Lady Cadman happy, take a few drill half-hours and oversee the permanent staff so that the hostel was kept clean and always ready for an inspection. In the rest room, a large salon overlooking the garden was the family's grand piano, left for our use.

From then on, young as I was, just nineteen years old, I found myself in a caring occupation, always working for the distaff side of the RAF. Luckily I was never posted to a Recruits Centre, but on each subsequent move was given a completely new post, always new things to learn and digest, often working entirely alone with responsibility for the welfare of girls of all types, some of them very young and vulnerable. I vividly remember some of the incidents that happened and the faces of some of the people I met are still quite clear in my memory.

The first lady that impressed me was our Commandant, Katherine Jane Trefusis Forbes, who gave a welcome and lecture on the recruits course at Innsworth. My husband remembers me saying she had 'piercing blue eyes'; I was very impressed with her smartness and bearing.

At HQFC (HQ Fighter Command) I often saw Winston Churchill and other dignitaries arriving for conferences in the Mansion and once, when Orderly Corporal one evening, I went to the Underground Ops room with the Orderly Officer, who was a Code and Cypher Officer. She wanted something from her office and insisted I went with her, although I told her I hadn't a pass and was not allowed underground. Coming back up the slope from underground after watching the Ops girls at work I noticed some American Officers striding down towards us.

"Don't take any notice," the Officer said, but I did raise my eyes and saw General Eisenhower watching me as they neared us. I was in a panic, wondering if he would guess I hadn't a pass and I would be in serious trouble, but he strode on past us and I breathed again.

As I was Admin, I was also answering to Mrs Brimblecombe, the WAAF Station Warrant Officer (known as "Mrs B") and could be sent on escort duties to pick up absconders when they were discovered. One trip was to South West Wales. Two girls always went together, an NCO and an airwoman holding the same rank as the deserter. Train journeys could be quite painful in those days; no heating in carriages, no food of course, we had to pick up some sandwiches at the cookhouse to take with us, and it was a long and cold journey to Haverfordwest. Sometimes trains could be stopped for minutes at a time to let a troop train pass first. Only the trains on long journeys had corridors and lavatories, smaller local trains had single, separate carriages, no corridors, and once in one had to stay until reaching a station. Station names had been removed from the platforms, signposts too, so that a German spy would not know where he was. That went for us too, and if you couldn't hear the name of the station when it was shouted out, you could be anywhere! It now occurs to me if it was thought a German spy would be deaf or couldn't speak English!

It was dark when we reached our destination and we were met by an RAF driver with a lorry to take us to the RAF Station. Sitting in the back with some airmen who had also been picked up, we seemed to go for miles down country lanes, unable in the dark to pick out any landmarks, only seeing black trees as we flashed past, until we got to a Nissen hutted camp. We were given a bed in one hut for the night and next morning found that the girl we had come to escort back to BP had escaped their vigilance and disappeared. Mrs B was furious, telling me later the station had lost the girl three days earlier but had hoped to pick her up again before I arrived, and she hadn't been informed before I left to go there.

It transpired that the girl had married a local man, a civilian, and, missing him, had absconded. I empathised with her; I missed my husband too.

On another occasion, Mrs B sent me to the WAAF Police department at West Kensington to pick up a girl who had deserted and found by them without a leave pass. I was to go home with the girl to pick up her kit and endeavour to find out what the family situation was and come back with her to give my report. I cannot remember the area, but it had been very severely bombed all around. I found all her family there except for her young brother, who was not yet home from school. Her father and mother were worried about their daughter and asked me what would happen to her. I reassured them that nothing too terrible would occur, but that she would be confined to camp. Her mother was in a terrible state of nerves. She and the young son had been evacuated, but her husband had remained in London because of his work. Worry over his safety had caused her and the boy's return to London, where the bombing and continuing worry about his journey to and from school and her husband's to his work, did not help her state of mind.

I reported this to Mrs B on our return and it was then that I realised what a caring person she really was. The girl had to stay for a few days confined to camp and was then sent on two weeks compassionate leave to try and sort out her family worries.

But Mrs B would not tolerate any failure in duty by any of her own Admin staff, and after lecturing me for arriving late on parade one morning said she was sending me to Rochford on another escort duty. I was overjoyed, though tried not to show it.

My husband had been detached there from Hornchurch to take charge when their Signals Flight Sergeant went on leave, so we were able to walk around the camp talking our heads off all evening. Next morning I took charge of the prisoner (I had refused this duty the evening before) and returned to camp. I wonder now if somehow Mrs B found out from one of my friends that he was there and was being considerate once again.

Another Admin corporal on a similar trip came back with her prisoner, but her escort had deserted from Paddington station. I never heard what Mrs B said to her. It could be a worrying job watching the girl and even accompanying her to toilets, just in case she tried to bolt again.

Mrs B's clear and authoritative voice is the one I remember as well as the lady herself.

## A False Alarm

*Patricia Coulson*

At Uxbridge in 1943 we were billeted in married quarters. One evening a girl from the house next door rushed in saying 'Have you heard? We are all going to Baghdad, I heard them talking about it in the orderly room. The corporal will be along to tell us all about it. Baghdad? Did that mean tropical kit? Would we get leave? The corporal duly arrived and put us wise. The barrack blocks surrounding the parade ground bore foreign names, and we were to move into Baghdad *Block*.

No tropical kit, no special leave!

# The Biter Bit!

*Pam Daniels née Bennett*

When I was doing my square bashing at Morecambe in December 1941, one of the coldest winters of the war, I was in a billet on the sea front with six other raw (in every sense of the word) recruits. The tall, narrow terraced house had been a typical seaside boarding house before and had, until then, been the temporary home of RAF recruits and, my word, did the 'lady of the house' resent us.

We slept on the third floor in a large attic room which had several buckets and bowls to catch the drips when it rained. We were allowed to boil one kettle at 9pm to make our cocoa, but one of us kept guard each evening while another kettleful was boiled for our much needed hot water bottles.

One evening the landlady came into the kitchen just as one of us – ACW Sarah Oliver – was refilling the kettle for a second boil. "Oh no you don't!" she cried, snatching the kettle away and emptying it into the sink. One of the other girls then quietly said, "Well… now you will be able to boast that you refused the Prime Minister's daughter a hot water bottle!" (We had, at her request, kept Sarah's identity a secret until then.)

Sarah was offered the best guest-room on the first floor, carpeted and with a pink taffeta eiderdown, but she just gave the landlady a withering look and said she would prefer to stay with her friends.

I was eventually posted to Penarth to do my Pay Accounts course and Sarah went to Officer Training Unit and we lost touch.

# The Tale of a Clerk/GD

*B. Wilson*

It was springtime in 1941 when I arrived at Bridgnorth. After the weeks of kitting out, medicals, NAAFI tea and coming to terms with RAF cuisine, I was posted to No. 1 School of Technical Training, RAF Halton in Buckinghamshire, where there were many units; Aircraft Apprentices (called Brats), and, for a short period, Fleet Air Arm Apprentices, all of whom marched everywhere with their bagpipe band and Lewis the goat. There were also Flight Mech courses (A and E), conversion courses for fitters, School of Cookery, a small aerodrome and Princess Mary's RAF hospital.

The black huts from WW1 were our billets. SHQ was also a conglomeration of huts with kidney stoves and, in the snowy winter of 1941/42, we typed wearing mittens. The social life more than compensated and we were encouraged to actively participate in many sports which meant we could finish work early on Saturdays. Twelve of us moved from the huts into a semi in the WO's quarters near the hospital.

Later, two additional WAAF ranks were introduced, those of WO and LACW. After many hours poring over a copy of KRs and ACIs our Trade Test resulted in half a dozen of us becoming LACWs, flaunting our brand new props and getting a lot of teasing from the airmen.

Records detached me 'for duty only' to the hospital. My worst memories are of the various hospital 'pongs' coupled with the aroma of the patients' breakfasts, but a week later I didn't notice it. The next 18 months passed by fairly smoothly while working as secretary to the Wing Commander and Squadron Leader eye surgeons, plus taking notes at the daily out-patient clinics. Twice yearly we attended the new intake of would-be aircraft apprentices, and the colour-vision tests were my chore. After 300 of these I could read the wrong answers as well as the right ones on the Ishihara charts.

We once had a 300 strong intake of young Polish boys, all hoping to become apprentices, after a very arduous trek from the Russian-occupied part of Poland, via the USSR to Palestine and on to the UK. Knowing no Polish, a helpful Polish Nursing Orderly at the hospital wrote out phonetically the 'right' answers and the 'wrong'.

Another sideline was helping the wing commander to choose the correct colour of an artificial eye. I gazed into the airman's good eye and told 'Sir' when he'd got a colour match! An unusual task was collecting empty face cream jars for despatch to Professor Florey (assistant to Sir Alexander Fleming) in Oxford, who returned them filled with precious penicillin, still in its trial stage, for use in the Ophthalmic ward. Progress reports would be typed weekly and returned with the next batch of empty jars.

Records then posted me on an NCOs course from which I emerged as a corporal, with immediate despatch to the Orderly Room and a world of 36 hours on duty/or call, and with telegrams beginning 'Regret to inform you...' (a dozen death certificates after one crash), escorting next-of-kin to the mortuary and so on. It was not all gloom though, as in October 1943 we had 79 medical repatriations from Germany, and life took on a rosier hue, their antics keeping us amused, but causing a nightmare for our humourless Group Captain in charge.

Most of us looked upon the Sycamore Club in Amersham as our second home, open each day until midnight. We were fed, cosseted, invited to numerous parties and generally encouraged to forget our daily pressures.

In November 1944 came my one and only real posting, to another hospital in Ely. After the lovely Chiltern Hills, the freezing fog and mists rolling across the Fens, the Nissen huts and flooding duckboards in the ablutions came as quite a shock. But on the plus side, the hospital was very modern, we were treated well, the catering was the tops, and the genial atmosphere helped a great deal. Chronic understaffing meant twelve hour stints on duty several times a week, but we did finish at 5pm on Sundays. Two half days off per month was the norm, but the social life when we were off duty and not falling asleep on our feet, was varied, widespread and brilliant.

With the end of the war in Europe, life became easier, and we saw our friends reunited with husbands or fiancés returning from captivity in Germany. Which demob group number applied to us became a topic of conversation and speculation. Records posted me to Kirkham for a senior Clk/GD course, to be followed by another at Wilmslow. But luckily VJ-Day came and went, my demob number came up and in August 1945 I left the WAAF.

I certainly don't regret those years, but the foregoing is very much the other unglamorous side of the coin.

Our education was complete. We had learned to forge signatures on the 'duplicate' permanent passes we had 'borrowed' from the bottom of the pile, on the premise that we would be posted or the war would be over before our crime was discovered. We removed a few pages of cigarette coupons to fuel our ongoing battle with the NAAFI manageress. We spat on our fingers and retrieved the soap coupons we had just handed over, and we appropriated anything that was not nailed down.

I am still in touch with some friends from those days.

# Plotting the ships

*Eileen Richards née Rigby*

I think that the happiest year for me during my five in the WAAF was spent at RAF Thorpeness, a small radar unit on the Suffolk coast, just north of Aldeburgh. It was such a modest community, and we all knew each other well, being almost like a family. We girls lived in a lovely house almost on the shore. The airmen were in another house nearby, which they shared with the airmen who guarded us.

By 1943 we were able to plot shipping and this we carried out, plotting to Harwich. Every day a convoy came up the East Coast on a swept channel on the way to America. We had to watch out for stragglers who moved out of the channel and were thus likely to be blown up, or for E Boats trying to get in.

Also in daytime, the coastal forces who went on patrol across the North Sea to the Dutch coast. These were MTBs and MLs, and we plotted them over and watched for their return.

One night we were asked to look out for one group which were late back, and captained by Peter Scott. We did all this from echos on a radar screen and could give a pretty good idea of tonnage on the shipping.

Perhaps the most interesting few days were spent on an exchange visit to Harwich with some Wrens. There we worked in the Naval Pilot ship dealing with the results of our work at the other end of the line. The highlight that week was a visit to a Corvette, *HMS Shearwater*, in harbour there, whose captain was Nicholas Monserrat, author of the *The Cruel Sea* and many other books.

# A Shift to Remember

*Edna Frost née Emmett, Canada*

I was an LACW Teleprinter Operator from October 1942 to September 1946 and found service life interesting and exciting.

Stationed in various parts of Britain over the years, I had the good fortune to be in Lincolnshire in June 1944.

June 5th started out much as usual. Several of us were picked up in a jeep from RAF Spitalfields and taken to a US base a couple of miles away for our late afternoon shift. Signals was always a busy section, but seemed particularly hectic on this day, and we all felt an undercurrent of tension. Fingers flew fast and furious on the keys sending and receiving coded messages continuously.

We were not told anything specific, but it was apparent that something special was happening. Being caught up in the intensity of the work we were too busy for a coffee break. Time flew by and when it was time to end our shift the teleprinters were still clattering away. As our replacements had not arrived to relieve us, we just kept going. The WAAF Corporal in charge informed us we were to continue working and that coffee and doughnuts would be served to us at our teleprinters every hour on the hour by the American personnel on duty. I had never been a coffee drinker before, but was glad of the hot drinks, which helped to keep our adrenaline up.

After twelve hours of sending coded messages, our finger ends were numb and we were pleased to notice the intense pressure of work beginning to ease. When our relief arrived our corporal informed us that we were not to discuss anything with them; we were quickly ushered onto the transport which took us back to the RAF station. There a WAAF officer told us to go directly to the mess hall, and, although we all felt too weary to eat, we did as we were told. There the stupendous news was broken to us, the D-Day invasion had begun. Our weariness dropped away and we stood and cheered. It was a very proud and moving moment and we felt so pleased that we had contributed in some way towards the beginning of the end of the war.

Shortly after D-Day, the American unit where our signal section was based was transferred to 'somewhere in Europe'. The Commanding Officer personally thanked all the WAAF Teleprinter/Ops for the work we had done and said that if he could have taken us with them to Europe he would willingly have done so. It was a proud moment.

## An Innocent Abroad

*Val Malloy, Australia*

I remember when I was a very shy seventeen-year-old at Wilmslow I came out in a rash and was whisked off into sick quarters. Imagine my horror next morning when I was awakened by a man! I ducked under the bedclothes and would not come out until he had left. The poor RAF orderly could only repeat 'I didn't do anything… only bring her breakfast tray'.

I laugh now, but in my sheltered life I had never had a male see me in my night attire. And what night attire! WAAF issue blue and white striped cotton pyjamas.

Still, it was a time I was glad to be part of.

# D-Day at Croydon

*Barbara McMaster*

In 1943 I had joined the medical staff of Croydon Airport. Being part of Transport Command, with a constant stream of personnel in transit to overseas stations, we were very busy dealing with emergencies (a crashed Lancaster bomber on the airfield one day as we were serving supper and comforting anxious men.)

As spring 1944 approached we all sensed that 'something very big' was afoot, but security was tight and ours was not to question too closely. There was an atmosphere of expectation as we listened to the radio off duty. Never shall I forget the pounding beat of the Big Bands, whose melodies and romantic lyrics encapsulated the anticipation of the time. We jabbed the boys with inoculations, danced with them, hugged them and waved them goodbye...

On June 5th we lay sleepless on our beds with the incessant drone of aircraft passing overhead. In the moonlight we distinguished their sombre outlines. Glenn Miller was playing on the radio all night long.

Early next day we were summoned on parade in front of the main airport building, leaving just a skeleton staff on duty. Medical staff usually avoided formal parades so it was amusing to see us smartly turned out with shoes and buttons gleaming, lined up with many of our ex-patients on the tarmac.

The CO read a message from a VIP informing us that D-Day had begun, and exhorting us to do our duty and to be prepared for absolutely anything. You could have heard a pin drop!

We savoured our private thoughts. I thought about Ken fighting in Italy and breathed a sigh of thankfulness that he would not be crossing the channel to France.

During the ensuing weeks I learned the fate of many of our newly-acquired friends. It was a momentous time in our history, though poignant and tragic on personal levels. The girls kept on working, but with heavy hearts.

SUPREME HEADQUARTERS
ALLIED EXPEDITIONARY FORCE

Soldiers, Sailors and Airmen of the Allied Expeditionary Force!

You are about to embark upon the Great Crusade, toward which we have striven these many months. The eyes of the world are upon you. The hopes and prayers of liberty-loving people everywhere march with you. In company with our brave Allies and brothers-in-arms on other Fronts, you will bring about the destruction of the German war machine, the elimination of Nazi tyranny over the oppressed peoples of Europe, and security for ourselves in a free world.

Your task will not be an easy one. Your enemy is well trained, well equipped and battle-hardened. He will fight savagely.

But this is the year 1944! Much has happened since the Nazi triumphs of 1940-41. The United Nations have in-flicted upon the Germans great defeats, in open battle, man-to-man. Our air offensive has seriously reduced their strength in the air and their capacity to wage war on the ground. Our Home Fronts have given us an overwhelming superiority in weapons and munitions of war, and placed at our disposal great reserves of trained fighting men. The tide has turned! The free men of the world are marching together to Victory!

I have full confidence in your courage, devotion to duty and skill in battle. We will accept nothing less than full Victory!

Good Luck! And let us all beseech the blessing of Al-mighty God upon this great and noble undertaking.

Dwight D Eisenhower

Returning from duty at Bentley Priory in June 1944, airwomen found a copy of General Eisenhower's message had been placed on each bed.

# 2. Off Duty

Even during the darkest and most worrying days, youthful spirits came to the fore and we found ways of relaxing from tension. Cinemas were in the nearest and smallest of towns, even if the films were old ones. There was also, always the NAAFI, where one could order a plate of sausage and chips and enjoy the friendship of other girls, or invite the current airman boyfriend in, instead of wandering around the station in the cold. Dances were held there, also outside camp at the Town Hall, or one of the several volunteer canteens. Entertainment Officers could arrange concerts held by ENSA or those with experience of large city entertainment could gather together old friends to put on a show.

Fighter Command was fortunate to have Freddie Carpenter as their Entertainment Officer. Before he enlisted in the RAF he had been a well-known choreographer and dancer in the West End of London, with many friends, and he arranged one long-remembered show which featured well-known film stars of the day John Mills and Stewart Granger, Tessie O'Shea – a popular entertainer billed as 'Two-Ton Tessie' – and singer Gwen Catley. Musical evenings were held with well-known orchestras and soloists. Dances and concerts were also run by enthusiastic station personnel as many of them had ability in the acting field and could sing and dance well. Most stations ran a dance band as well as playing marching band music for the Sunday Church Parade, and had mixed airmen/women or a fife and drum marching band consisting entirely of WAAF personnel.

# The Wymeswold Dance Band

*Babs Forster née Sargent*

In February 1943, I was posted to RAF Wymeswold and served there for two years. As I was a musician and entertainer I joined a five-piece band consisting of a pilot instructor, a navigator instructor from New Zealand and a wireless operator, all on saxophone, an MT Driver on trumpet, and myself (WAAF admin) on piano and accordion. Corporal Disney, a flight mechanic and a double bass player, was in charge. We used to play for dances on camp and also around Loughborough.

The Wymeswold Concert Party, Babs centre.

Babs with her accordion

There were a lot of talented people around and we formed a concert party and choir with which we toured the area to raise funds for various causes. Eric Griffin wrote sketches, which we performed at various venues.

The PT College at Loughborough was being used as a rehabilitation centre and convalescent home and was run by a Polish doctor who had escaped with his wife from Poland. She was a brilliant pianist and often gave recitals. On many occasions we took our band and concert party there to entertain the patients.

Just before D-Day, all leave was cancelled and there were thousands of troops from many nations stationed in the area, waiting to go to the coast. Problems arrived when a 15-piece band, which had been scheduled to perform at the Town Hall, was unable to do so (they were all workers at the Royal Ordnance factory and had been put on double shifts).

A request for any musicians in the area to report to the Town Hall was sent around and we responded. It was quite an experience for me. Being a pianist, who also played the accordion for rumbas and so on, I never knew what nationalities would turn up at the dances but just tried to keep the troops happy and dancing. Of course, the Americans brought along all the latest jiving scores. It was brilliant!

# Those Wonderful WAAF Marching Bands

*Beryl Williams*

In the early years of the war, when many of our cities endured the 'Blitzkrieg' and the destruction of lives and homes, optimism and trust that the country would pull through eventually, had become a priority. A spirit of defiance and determination was engendered by those in command. It was crucial to keep morale high, and on RAF stations, as well as providing entertainment, commanding officers, RAF and WAAF, asked for volunteer musicians to form marching bands. Airwomen volunteering to become drummers or fife players were not all trained musicians, but, undeterred, they worked hard in their off-duty time, and regular musicians from RAF Uxbridge came to train them and become their bandmasters. It is not recorded how many WAAF bands there were, though over twenty-five have been researched, and as the success of the early bands was acknowledged, many other stations large enough to support one formed their own.

From 16MU Stafford in the North, down to RAF Pucklechurch in the West Country, the number of WAAF bands multiplied. Eventually the bands played not only for church parades, but also outside on many parades to help raise money for weapons, such as 'Wings for Victory', 'Support the Soldier', 'Thanks for Tanks', or at inter-services hockey matches and other sports functions, giving marching displays during the intervals. The newly-formed band at RAF Cottesmore was asked to lead a parade at Oakham. Their repertoire was slight and Joyce Chapman found the choice of music highly entertaining as the WAAF band led a 'Farm Day' parade to the strains of 'Life on the Ocean Wave'.

The airwomen who volunteered came from many different trades, although because of their shift-work and their acute

~ 113 ~

necessity to the well-being of the personnel, cooks were not always allowed. This was much to the dismay of Ellen Dance, a cook at No. 3 Balloon Centre who said, '…the band rehearsed in all weathers and the station was very proud of them. I would have loved to have taken part.'

Irene Milne née Gilchrist dusts off her cymbals in the desert at RAF Heliopolis.

The band of HQ 16 Group, Coastal Command, Gillingham. Drum major is Drum Sgt Goddard, Royal Marines. Peggy Badger stands behind the mace. 1943-44

Band practice in the open air.

Peggy Crole née Badger, right, with her sister Joyce Gibbens.

Joyce Knight née Duncan.

# The Service Dance Bands

The Royal Navy, Army and RAF had their own dance bands, and many musicians in these bands were from famous pre-war dance bands which had played regularly for West End balls, broadcasting frequently on the radio. The RAF formed No.1 Dance Band, which came to be known as The Squadronnaires, another was the Skyrockets, a band originally formed at the Balloon Centre at Wythall. All the British service bands were as gifted as the evergreen and celebrated American Army Air Force band led by Glenn Miller whose melodic swing music captured a devoted following. We danced as we listened to the sentimental words:

> *The touch of your lips upon my brow*
> *The love in your eyes that shine*
>
> *Be careful it's my heart*
> *Its not my note your'e holding*
> *It's my heart.*
>
> *I'm making believe that you're in my arms*
> *Though I know that you're far away*

There were many other songs in a similar vein. We listened to Anne Shelton on the radio, Vera Lynn, who sang with a sob in her voice and became 'The Forces Sweetheart', and many other singers. But there were also some more upbeat songs:

> *You are my sunshine, my only sunshine*
> *You make me happy when skies are grey*
> *You'll never know dear*
> *How much I love you*
> *Please don't take my sunshine away.*

There were plenty of other songs such as There'll be Bluebirds over the White Cliffs of Dover; Kiss me Goodnight Sergeant Major; We're Going to Hang Out Our Washing on the Siegfried Line; In the Mood; and so many others – all with lyrics that we would sing as we returned together from a birthday celebration or a dance. And there were silly songs such as 'Run Rabbit Run', 'Mairzie Doats' and countless others.

Naturally the WAAF girls soon learned the words of the songs the airmen sang, and it took one aback to hear young girls arm in arm with their RAF escort coming back from a dance or the cinema along the country lanes singing heartily,

*Roll me over in the clover*
*Roll me over, lay me down, and do it again!*

Perhaps the suggestive words of this type of song went over the heads of the younger airwomen!

# An artist in the WAAF

*Beryl Williams*

At the age of 34, Elva Blacker, a photographer and painter, having driven an ambulance for the Blood Donor organisation, enlisted in the WAAF in 1942 as an MT Driver and was stationed at Biggin Hill.

Elva Blacker

She had already achieved recognition for her art and had sketched and painted many artists in the acting profession, accepting portrait commissions, including from the actresses Gladys Cooper, Dame Sybil Thorndike and Nina, Duchess of Hamilton and Brandon, and had also painted a miniature of George Bernard Shaw. Her miniatures were considered to be among her best work, though her versatility encompassed many expressions of art.

At first at Biggin Hill, Elva drove ambulances, but later became driver for the Intelligence Officer. Colleagues remember that Elva was always sketching. She picked her subjects, asking them to sit for her, and worked her sketches into portraits, always photographing them and giving a photo to her sitter.

Renney by Elva Blacker 1943

Her subjects ranged from RAF and WAAF ground crew, chaplains, ops rooms and aircrew from many countries, including Australia, South Africa, Canada, Poland and Czechoslovakia and Free French pilots. Her vegetarian diet (vegetarians being looked upon at that time as 'cranks') must have been difficult to follow, but she is remembered as a good-natured person with boundless energy and for always having tomatoes and apples in her locker and a stick of celery poking out from a pocket.

Her study of pilots at a debriefing session was exhibited and Queen Elizabeth discussed the painting with her when she visited Biggin Hill.

Elva at work

Elva was later posted to RAF Manston where she drove, painted and sketched pilots of No. 91 Squadron. She attended an Education Vocational Training course, was promoted to Sergeant and then posted as an Instructor in art at two other RAF stations.

Many examples of Elva's wartime work are held in the archives at the RAF Museum, Hendon – a unique record of the men and women who served in those days of strife. Two exhibitions have recently been mounted by the Museum; in 2002 at RAF Cosford and in 2003 at Hendon.

WAAF MT Drivers rest room, Biggin Hill 1943 by Elva Blacker.

234 SQUADRON 124 SQUADRON

**ROYAL AIR FORCE**
**BENTWATERS**
**11 GROUP, FIGHTER COMMAND.**

Officer Commanding :
Wing Commander P. B. LUCAS, D.S.O., D.F.C.

## Menu for Christmas Day 1945.

. 239

### Menu.

**SOUPS**
Cream of Tomato    Consomme

**POULTRY**
Roast Turkey    Bread Sauce
Roast Surrey Fowl    Sage and Onion Stuffing

**JOINTS**
Roast Loin of Pork    Apple Sauce

**VEGETABLES**
Boiled and Baked Potatoes
Boiled and Baked Parsnips
Cauliflower    Brussels Sprouts

**SWEETS**
Christmas Pudding    Mock Rum Cream
Mince Pies
Cheese and Biscuits
Dessert Fruit
Coffee
Beer and Lemonade, Etc.
Cigarettes

*Message from the Station Commander to All Ranks.*

"For the first time in six years we can eat our Christmas Dinner in peace

This excellent state of affairs is due in large measure to each one of you, and to the efforts which you have made across these last fateful years.

From Berlin to Alamein, from Normandy to the Timor Sea, the R.A.F. in close company with the Royal Navy, the Army and our Allies, have absolutely and utterly destroyed the enemy.

And now that peace reigns once more let us give thanks for the blessings which are ours.

A Merry Christmas to each one of you and a Prosperous New Year to you all."

*Lucas.*

Wing Commander, Commanding
R.A.F. Station, Bentwaters.

25th December, 1945.

The first peacetime Christmas dinner menu from RAF Bentwaters, signed by the famous air ace Laddie Lucas. (Menu from Mabel Wallace)

# 3. *Wartime Romance*

It was inevitable that with young airmen and women working closely together, romance would be in the air, and weddings planned. Sadly, not all took place. An aircrew bridegroom-to-be sometimes did not survive operations or was posted overseas before the wedding could take place. But many happy unions did occur, either at the local church, or on leave at home with family around. Clothing coupons were not issued to WAAF, and so wedding dresses were hard to come by unless coupons were forthcoming from generous families, or dresses were borrowed. But as time went on, agencies were set up where a service girl could borrow a wedding dress. Film studios would lend a dress that had been worn in a film by a well-known actress, asking only for a small sum to cover any cleaning charges.

With food rationing, cakes were also scarce, but lucky the girl whose older sister had saved a tier from her own wedding, and donated it to her, or had a family who rallied around and donated their sugar ration to help.

So despite difficulties, some weddings did take place, as related in the next story by Dorothy Woodford...

# A D-Day Marriage

*Dorothy Woodford, Leicester*

During those eventful days when plans were being laid for D-Day, I was stationed a few miles from the East Coast at Bircham Newton. My plans included marriage in June.

We had heard rumours of an invasion and a weekend trip home showed this to be possibly more imminent than we had imagined. Three of us hitch-hiked home to the Midlands. By midnight we were sitting on the steps of the Mermaid Hotel at Wansford, hoping for another lift, when we heard a steady rumble of traffic and a huge convoy of army vehicles, tanks, transporters, made its way in front of our eyes. It was an awesome sight as we sat silently watching its slow progress.

On our return to camp we learned that all leave was cancelled for an indefinite period. This was a blow, as I had planned to make more trips home to try on my half-made wedding dress of coupon-free lace from Leicester market and finalise arrangements. Letters to and from home arrived with pieces cut out by the censor, although I gathered my poor mother was frantic, not knowing whether the wedding was on or off.

I plucked up courage to approach the senior WAAF Officer, who was sympathetic but adamant that leave was quite out of the question. I thought of the half-made plans, the wedding cake made by mother after months of hoarding the ingredients, the borrowed trousseau from WAAF friends. We had a system, several of us having wedding plans, by which our few civilian clothes did the rounds. I was on the list to borrow a camel coat and summer dress, and these were already earmarked for another girl on my return from honeymoon.

My spirits were at zero when the officer said, that although I could not have leave, she was prepared to excuse my duties for ten days, the implication being that it was my responsibility what I did with this unexpected offer. With help from a couple of RAF Regiment boys I left camp in the back of a lorry containing machine-guns, and got through the camp gates without trouble. In King's Lynn I made my way to the YWCA and changed into 'civvies' before hitching to Leicester, keeping a look-out for Military Police.

In church next day I was to find the best man was on his way to the Far East, the reserve to Iceland and a perfect stranger stood next to my husband-to-be. We left for our honeymoon in Lynmouth. The guest-house proprietor asked for our ration cards. Not having a leave pass, I was without one which did not go down with him very well. Fortunately, while walking by the river the next day, we disturbed a poacher, and there, lying on the bank, was a freshly caught salmon. With this wrapped in my husband's jacket, there were no more questions about ration cards, all was sweetness. We even had a £2 reduction on our bill!

# My Wartime Wedding

*Jean Copeland née Ratcliffe, Tilehurst*

Reg, a Royal Engineer, and I, a WAAF at RAF Benson , were engaged and decided to wait until the war ended before getting married. But in early 1945 Reg was told he would be posted overseas, when and where not known, so we thought we would marry before he went.

We fixed the date for 30th April, the cake was made and other arrangements sorted out. The banns had been called twice in Ewelme Church when out of the blue came a telegram. *'On embarkation leave, can you make the wedding next Saturday?'*

There was a bit of a panic but the forecasters and meteorological assistants rallied round to help. I rushed home to London to get some civilian clothes and then had to dash to Oxford to arrange for a special license. (Reg was in Scotland). I contacted a Justice of the Peace, and all Reg had to do was sign, pay and take the license to the Rector. Before he left Scotland he was given all his overseas jabs in one go, spent two days ill in bed and was then considered fit to travel. He was put on a train, and the guard instructed to make sure he got off at Crewe, his home town. Later, on arrival in Oxford, he had lost my instructions about the JP but somehow managed to obtain a license from another one. (I had to explain all this to my mystified JP on my return who wondered why the license had not been collected. He was amused and sympathetic and would only accept payment for the stamp duty).

Audrey, a Met Assistant, who had married a few months earlier, lent me her wedding dress, and the Rector's wife, her veil. I think the other clothes were mine! Reg's brother was to be best man, but sadly had a hernia, so another brother took over. My brother, who gave me away, came straight off night duty in a factory in London, and getting to Benson and the church was no light matter for him in those days.

Clippings from the office punch machine made the confetti, and the village children threw wild flower heads over us. An American officer in nearby Mount Farm had given a bottle of champagne to one of our forecasters who generously made it into a 'punch' so that everyone had a sip. Since RAF Benson was a Photo Reconnaissance Unit, we were able to borrow some film and a cameraman. I was told afterwards that a Spitfire or Mosquito flew over the church and drowned out my "I will". (We celebrated our Golden Wedding Anniversary in New Zealand where our son now lives.)

# If You Can't Cook, Marry a Chef!

*Joyce Barnard née Hugget, Hounslow*

Not everyone can cook, they have to be taught. There were few really good ones around but I married one. Peter was a Corporal cook in the cookhouse at Gloucester but had been a chef before joining the RAF. We married by special licence at Barnwood in 1944, and spent a three-day honeymoon before Peter's embarkation leave was over. It was a white wedding with a WAAF Guard of Honour, everything borrowed. Even the £15 Peter borrowed from his sister, which was the final cost of the wedding (and that included my wedding ring £3, Licence £2.10, the car, sandwiches, a bottle of whisky on sale or return and any extras.) And I remember the wedding cake, a present from the cookhouse staff, made with wartime ingredients, which fell to bits as soon as it was cut.

But it didn't matter, we were in love and married and I was absolutely sure that Peter would come back to me safely from overseas … and so he did, after two years, and we have had a wonderful life together.

# A Marriage that Nearly Wasn't

*Anne and Peter Osborne*

Anne and Peter met at Northcotes in 1944, married at the local church on 9th June. The day before, Anne fell off her bike and badly damaged her kneecap and was taken to sick quarters. Next day, still with a sore knee, Anne and Peter, with Bob, best man, and friends all waited at the church, but no Padre appeared. Bob jumped on his bike and cycled to the vicarage where he found the Padre sitting down to a quiet lunch without a care in the world. He had put the wrong date in his diary!

Bob prised him from his chair and nearly an hour late the wedding began. There was no time left for a reception, and four days later Peter and Bob were detached to RAF Manston for further operations in the Channel area.

The wedding of Anne and Peter Osborne with L-R Tate, Burgess, Padre Howard, Bob, Peter and Anne, Furnish, Gilmore and Maureen.

# Wartime Love Knew No Borders

The war brought the opportunity for girls to meet young servicemen from many overseas countries. Travel opportunities in the days before the war were not readily available for most people, and so these meetings would otherwise not have taken place. Many girls, especially those working on operational units, married airmen from Poland, Australia, Canada, South Africa, Czechoslovakia and France, among others. When the war was over they joined their husbands in their respective homelands and their journeys to do so were often their first time abroad. It was a great wrench for some of them to leave their families and all that was familiar and dear to them to live in a new country among people who spoke and lived in ways that were different from their own experience.

**Audrey Rice** tells of her 1946 travel as a war bride and widow to Canada in the *Queen Mary*, which was used as a troopship. With her she took her infant son Derek. His father, Rene Gillette, a pilot in the Royal Canadian Air Force, lost his life in a flight over England in early 1945. Leaving her family in England, Audrey settled in Ottawa, Ontario, with her son (now grown with two sons of his own).

Audrey and Derek with their memento, The Queen Mary.]

But for some girls, leaving a loving family was too much. Fearing she would never see her mother again if she went to Australia to marry her fiancé, one girl called off her engagement. But she never forgot the first man she had loved and, many years later on a visit to Australia she was able to track him down. She discovered from his wife that he had never forgotten his first love either. Although he was now old and balding, in her eyes he was still the handsome young pilot she had fallen in love with.

# As One Waaf To Another

*By Rebe Whittle, written on night duty in Ops Room, RAF Scampton 1942*

Oh, do not fall for a pilot tall
My bonny little WAAFY.
And that goes too, for the rest of the crew
You may dance with in the NAAFI
If you give your heart it will fall apart
When the crews take off at night.
So don't be a fool but play it cool
And they'll come back all right.

You'll only cry if you love a guy
Who's equally fond of you.
For you well know as you see him go
That he's got a heartache too.
Can't you just be friends until the war ends
Wait, without fret or fuss?
No, my dear, and nor I fear
Can he or the rest of us!

# 4. International relations

*Over There* was a pamphlet issued by the US War Department in 1942 to American servicemen who were going to Britain to prepare for the invasion of Europe. Many of these young men had never been abroad before and the aim was to prepare them for life in a different country and to try to prevent any friction with the local populace. One paragraph reads:

## BRITISH WOMEN AT WAR

*A British woman officer or non-commissioned officer can – and often does – give orders to a man private. The men obey smartly and know it is no shame. For British women have proven themselves in this way. They have stuck to their posts near burning ammunition dumps, delivered messages afoot after their motorcycles have been blasted from under them. They have pulled aviators from burning planes. They have died at the gun posts and as they fell another girl has stepped directly into the position and 'carried on.'*

*There is not a single record in this war of any British woman in uniformed service quitting her post or failing in her duty under fire.*

*Now you understand why British soldiers respect the women in uniform. They have won the right to the utmost respect. When you see a girl in khaki or air-force blue with a bit of ribbon on her tunic – remember she didn't get it for knitting more socks than anyone else in Ipswich.*

# Pour la patrie

*by M. Irene Park*

'Pour la patrie' it read.
So poignantly it said
It all.

For whose homeland? – not theirs;
And yet they helped us through that crucial time
By sea, on land and in the air
How many in that thin blue line*
Were Poles?
One in twelve – at one point one in ten, they say,
Only with their help did we live
To fight another day.
While then, as now, their land is subject to an alien will.
'Pour la patrie' – how much we owe them still.

*Written many years after the war, on seeing these words on the tombstone of a Polish pilot killed while flying with the RAF in 1944.)*

# The Polish WAAF

*From WINGS, periodical of the Polish Air Force Association, June 1944, Issue 144/630. Reproduced with permission of the PAFA Charitable Trust.*

The exploits of the Polish aircrew who served in this country are legendary. However, little is heard of their compatriots, the Polish women who joined the WAAF.

Many of these women had undergone great suffering before arriving in this country, had received no news of their families in Poland, and some could not speak English. Despite this, they played a very successful part in the national war effort.

It was on September1st 1939 that the German army invaded Poland from the west; two weeks later the Soviet Army invaded from the east. In this zone many Polish men and women were seized as 'political offenders' and deported to labour camps in Siberia and other remote areas. They were put to work on farms, in hospitals and given other menial work. Conditions were harsh, food was inadequate, and many were broken in health or else died.

In June 1941 Germany attacked the Soviet Union, which then entered the war on the side of the Allies. In return for Allied support, the Russians agreed to an amnesty, and the deportees were released. Six hundred miles to the east of Moscow a rallying centre for the Polish women was set up, and they trudged on foot hundreds of miles to reach it, arriving utterly exhausted by the hard journey.

Some of these girls were to reach the Middle East where, until 1943, they served with General Anders' Polish Army. It was then decided that they should be allowed to join the WAAF and be trained for duties with the Polish Air Force. Thirty-six women were enrolled in June 1943 and sent to Wilmslow for initial training. These were to act as instructors for the subsequent recruits. English lessons were given, then an NCOs course and twelve of these initial recruits were sent to the Officers' Training School at RAF Windermere, to be followed later by others.

Most of the recruits came, via Russia and the Middle East, from Eastern Poland, others came from Europe, Africa, India, Canada and the USA. Their ages ranged from 17 ½ to 43 years, and several mothers and daughters served together.

They enrolled as British WAAF and wore the same style uniform, but in mid-1944 royal assent was given to their wearing buttons and cap badges showing the Polish eagle, plus "Poland" shoulder flashes. All trades were open to them and after training, they were posted to duties in twenty-six PAF units, (where one in ten was a woman) thereby releasing British WAAF to serve elsewhere. But a few Polish WAAF served very well on British units, despite language difficulties.

The girls were very proud to be WAAF, worked hard during their training and took great care over their appearance. 1,436 airwomen served in the Polish WAAF, including 52 officers, and 110 NCOs , representing 10% of the total PAF in Great Britain. Some of these WAAF emigrated after the war, but most remained in this country. Efforts were made to contact their families left behind in Poland but, sadly, some never were able to find out what had happened to them.

The Polish Air Force Association (now disbanded) had a WAAF section consisting of all ranks, with its own annually elected committee.

*(With thanks to the late Alicja Kalienecka, Chairman PAFA WAAF Section and Betty Clements for providing the information used in this article.)*

# Serving with a PAF Squadron

*Joyce Szwagiel née Hughes*

In the autumn of 1943 I was posted to Snailwell in Suffolk, a Fighter Command unit, manned principally by a Polish Mustang Squadron, No. 309.

This was my first contact with members of our close and staunch allies, of whom I had heard little in my previous two years of service. I wondered what was in store for me when, on my first day, the orders issuing over the tannoy were in this strange language. I was a Pay Accounts clerk, and the Polish Accounts sergeant and corporal worked alongside us and were our translators. Their English was good, if a little fractured at times, and we worked harmoniously together.

But it was the ground crews who made our lives interesting and eventually made us very grateful to all these young men and the hundreds of other of their compatriots who stood shoulder to shoulder with us through these terrible times.

Eventually I met and married a Polish soldier who had been 5½ years a prisoner of war in Germany. His parents were still alive but warned him not to return to Poland under any circumstances. Because of hostility shown to him and others like him, he emigrated to the USA where I later joined him. After 1939 he never saw his parents again.

I have never forgotten the boys of No.309 Polish Squadron.

# America Honours a WAAF

An RAF corporal, now living in Australia sends an intriguing story concerning a WAAF, ACW I.G. Leask, on watch duty at Rosemount House, Prestwick. He tells of a night in late 1943 or early 1944 when he was corporal of the watch and the LACW, whom he calls 'Ella', was on Listening Command Guard, the SOS channel. She was a reliable girl, one of the best on the watch, he says.

On one particular night she heard a very faint sound and immediately called the corporal over. The sound turned out to be from an American squadron routed from the United States via Newfoundland and Reykjavik. Their leader had decided they would by-pass Reykjavik and fly straight across to Prestwick, and now the aircraft were running out of fuel. They were traced and found to be over Ireland, where a landing would possibly have ended in the crew's internment.

An aircraft was despatched to find and guide them over the water to Scotland and they all landed safely at Prestwick. Here they requested a meeting with the 'wonderful' girl who had heard their SOS and thus saved their lives. Ella was embarrassed to find herself hugged by so many American airmen.

A few weeks later word came that LACW Leask had been nominated to receive the US Legion of Merit. In February 1944 the *Sunday Times* newspaper published a photograph of US General Spatz pinning the medal onto her tunic and the caption read; 'LACW Leask, WAAF, for, as the citation and certificate of President Roosevelt stated, she was materially responsible for saving the lives of officers and men of a US formation which had become lost at sea.'

# Posted to Palestine

*Jean McMillan*

I enlisted in the WAAF, aged 17 years, from my home town of Chard in Somerset and was sent to Morecambe for basic training and then to Blackpool for the wireless course which lasted for six months. My first posting as a Wireless/Operator was to Ramsey on the Isle of Man, intercepting enemy coded signals underground. After this, I travelled north to Inverness where, in icy conditions, I tested radios in small aircraft. Fortunately it was only for three weeks, thus avoiding pneumonia!

I was posted to Bishops Court in Ireland in 1943 where the work was mundane, but I was thrilled to fly for the first time ever, and viewed the Mountains of Mourne from various angles as the pilot demonstrated his skill.

By this time I was longing for an overseas posting and after a three-week voyage on the *Winchester Castle*, I was fortunate enough to land in a Transit camp in Egypt, and from there to the most coveted destination, the Holy Land. So in August 1945 I arrived at the RAF staging post at Lydda (now Ben Gurion airport), 50 miles from Jerusalem. There were nine of us on each wireless watch and we were in contact by Morse code with many Middle Eastern airfields. It was the most satisfying work and we loved it.

Palestine in 1945 was beautiful, just like in Biblical times, and it was here in that wonderful land that I met my husband, Daniel, who also worked at Lydda as an RAF Flight/Mechanic E. We were married in September 1946 in the Dormition Abbey on Mount Zion in Jerusalem, Fifty years later we returned there to celebrate our Golden Wedding Anniversary and re-take our vows.

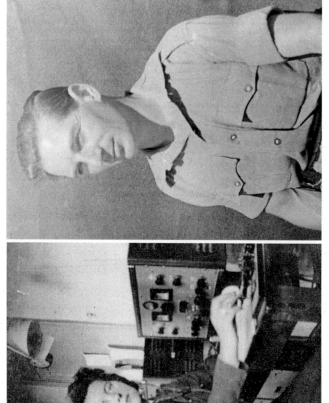

Jean McMillan née Joyce and husband Daniel, 1945

# Serving with the American Air Force

*Janet Giblin*

In 1943, serving as a Clerk/GD in the Orderly room of an RAF hospital, I was summoned by my sergeant and told I had been posted. This was a surprise in itself, but even more surprising was the fact that my posting was secret! Why would a lowly Clerk/GD be sent on a secret posting?

The answer came a few days later when reporting to the Admin Officer at the given address. I found I was to work at the headquarters of the Allied Expeditionary Air Force (AEAF), whose purpose was to plan their participation in the invasion of Normandy. Secret work indeed. The army and navy had their allied headquarters at other places, and together we served directly under the command of General Eisenhower's Supreme HQ or SHAEF. Our Air Force HQ office was located in a requisitioned house called Kestrel Grove, in Stanmore.

Being 'allied' meant that members of the WAAF and RAF worked alongside members of the American Air Force, and this proved to be interesting. A great sense of comradeship was quickly established as we learned about life in our respective countries. We British were fortunate as we were granted the privilege of using the American PX stores, which were stocked with cigarettes, chocolate, canned goods and lots of other goodies unobtainable in the NAAFI or shops in Britain at the time. Some of our American friends wrote home and asked their families to send make-up, nylons, soap and other special items which they gave us, always sharing their parcels from home.

The purpose of HQ AEAF was to provide gliders to transport troops to the invasion landing beaches, fighter planes to provide air cover to the troopships crossing the Channel, and all the equipment and supplies needed to support the invasion force. It was a masterpiece of organisation.

After D-Day, when the force was established in France, our HQ was moved to Bushy Park as SHAEF HQ had moved to France. Life there proved to be even better than at Stanmore; it was like living in a dream during those days of rationing, empty shops and RAF dining hall meals. Here, the meals were a wonderful sight; meat, vegetables, fruit, cream cakes – all kinds of goodies we had not seen for years and there was always the PX!

There was a shuttle bus service operating from the park for our convenience with a regular schedule to London, so we could always pop up there when off duty. No more waiting for buses and trains ... and no more worrying about being late back.

There was plenty of entertainment; the ballroom was huge and when we danced to Glenn Miller and his orchestra, we thought we were the luckiest girls in the WAAF.

Just after D-Day I was again posted and had to leave my American friends, those happy-go-lucky, generous young men who had shared their bounty with us and with whom we had shared our air raids and buzz-bombs.

My next move was to Germany where I joined BAFO (British Air Forces of Occupation), located in a schloss at Buckeburg. Another interesting posting, as our purpose was to disarm the remains of the German Air Force, so I was once again with my British comrades.

The war years were dreadful and yet enlightening to those of us in the services. We were given the opportunity of meeting people from all walks of life and many parts of the world, which enabled us to broaden our horizons in ways not dreamed of before. I consider myself very fortunate to have served with the WAAF and have a wealth of happy memories.

# Long Ago and Far Away

*Iris Sheppard née Burlingham*

In 1944 a small contingent of WAAF sailed from UK in order to establish bases for airwomen in India and Ceylon. Following this first sailing two troopships set sail from Liverpool, each carrying about 200 airwomen. The adventure began when we joined these ships, not knowing where we were going, but tropical kit had been issued to us, with suitable undies and topees, so it would seem we would be sailing into the sun. The reason for our postings to the Far East was to carry out duties and relieve airmen due for repatriation. The ship's quarters were crammed with troops, and mepacrine and quinine were forced upon us. No one seemed to care about the danger we could be in from the enemy. A real spirit of adventure had begun.

We were enchanted by India and Ceylon's beauty and the wonderful weather, mosques and palaces, elegant women in dazzling saris, and shops full of things we had not seen for years. A culture shock indeed. Unforgotten are the sunsets in their rapid, spectacular, way, croaking frogs, beautiful fireflies, the horrendous monsoons and the extreme poverty, and Arak Punch, the local drink. We particularly remember the dhobi wallahs who washed and starched our KD uniforms, sleeping on Charpoys with mosquito nets hanging over, coping with cockroaches, geckoes, weevils in bread and bugs of all sorts. Some of us suffered dengue fever and malaria, but once recovered and able to travel, we went up country to convalesce or on holiday to rest houses and tea plantations. We worked hard, and often were whirled into a frenzy of parties and all forms of entertainment and sport.

Colombo was a human hive. The WAAF site was nearby and within walking distance of our place of work, The Secretariat.

There was Mount Lavinia, a favourite spot for swimming, fresh pineapples, and passing trains always crammed with local people inside, outside, and on top of carriages. An incredible sight.

After VE and VJ days, troopships began to arrive in Colombo and flying boats into Koggala carrying our POWs. We were asked to look after them as best we could, such sad, poor souls who had suffered dreadfully at the hands of the Japanese.

Many servicewomen volunteered to go further afield and so it was we landed in Singapore and Hong Kong. In Singapore we were originally based in Tanglin Barracks, experiencing a creepy feeling to think the Japanese had used those barracks before us. Mostly we worked in large civilian buildings in the city centre and eventually were transferred to Changi. Singapore was trying to get back to normal and there was a mountain of work to be done, especially with War Crime tribunals being set up. It was an interesting time for all of us.

Repatriation came in due course and we look back and are proud of our service in the Far East. It evokes great memories and was special in so many ways. All that was long ago and far away, but the memories linger.

# Overseas with 2<sup>nd</sup> TAF

*Betty Woodin née Bladen*

I was a Corporal Clk/GD (Tech) stationed at HQFC Bentley Priory, then posted in April 1944 to HQ 85 Group at Uxbridge. The Group was the first contingent of WAAF to be posted to Normandy after D-Day, was originally formed as a Night Fighter Group and was later responsible for the recovery of crashed aircraft on the continent.

I worked for the Chief Engineering Officer and we had Technical Representatives attached to us. These 'tech reps' wore uniform, but were engineers from aircraft firms in the UK and USA whose responsibility was to make sure that any of their aircraft which we were operating arrived and were functioning and maintained correctly.

I remember typing stencils for 'Operation Overlord', every item preceded by 'D+' and a figure. Little did I know then what this meant and that I was typing the phasing-in instructions for the Group's aircraft and equipment to go to the Continent after D-Day. For security, these stencils had to be locked away each night, their safe place being a wooden stationery cupboard.

About 35 WAAFs were posted in, all different trades, and we shared the top floor of Somme Block with members of the WAAC of the USAAF. These girls wore their tin hats in the shower, and whereas we had grey lisle stockings, they had rows of nylons draped over the radiators. But they were a great bunch and we got on well together.

In August we had medicals and were kitted out with battledress, oilskins, sea boots, thick sea boot stockings, mess tins and so on and given a short leave. Although due to leave for Normandy on 15<sup>th</sup> September 1944 this was cancelled and we left the following week. It was intended we should go by Dakota, but these were 'frozen' for use in the Arnhem landings, so we were sent by sea. Because of this change, we were put into the hold of a Landing Ship Infantry (LSI), which was actually the Belgian cross-channel steamer, *Princess Astrid.*

What a night we spent! Cpl Babs Banks and I were told to sleep at the foot of the stairs in case any soldiers decided to venture below decks. We were not afraid of the soldiers, nor the enemy, but the cockroaches which milled around the stairs, and two rats which we saw on someone's ration bag! What a relief when morning came and we went back on deck. We were in a big convoy, balloons flying, the sea a magnificent blue and white.

As we came closer to Arromanches we transferred to a Landing Craft Tank (LCT) and as we approached the Mulberry Harbour, saw German prisoners of war on the quay, waiting to be sent to England. There was a hushed silence. As we disembarked and made our way to our transport we had a fantastic welcome from other members of the services.

We travelled through Bayeux and Caen to St Croix de Grande Tonne to our camp in the grounds of a house called Bon Acceuil, which became the WAAF mess and sick quarters. We slept in tents in the orchard, where apples dropped on us and chickens clucked outside. Ablutions were in the open and I remember one morning washing in my mess tin (shortage of water I think). The offices were in the buildings of the cider factory – very primitive, but clean.

After duty we were allowed to go outside the camp. All the roads were taped off because the ground on each side was mined. We always had to have an escort. The only place we could go to was a little café where Madame served us Calvados by the light of a lamp which she took into the next room when going to serve others, leaving us in total darkness.

We were in Normandy for about ten days and then flown in an Anson of 85 Group Communication Flight from Carpiquet (an airstrip close by) to Ghent in Belgium. As we flew over some French channel ports we saw them still burning. On the port side I saw our RAF bombers going on a 'thousand-bomber raid' and suddenly, from nowhere, fighter aircraft began circling them. I thought "this is it", but nothing happened, so they must have been ours.

In Ghent we were billeted in three houses and at last could have a proper wash and bath, but the plumbing in these houses never seemed to operate properly. One night water was cascading over the balcony into the hallway; it was actually coming up the plug-hole in the bath!

Fighting was still going on in Blankenberg and other pockets and we could hear the gunfire. We were given a tremendous welcome by the Belgian people and were invited to many homes. Flags were out everywhere.

The offices in what had been a hospital or nursing home had been occupied previously by the German organisation TODT[2] and backed onto an airstrip. At first there was no food; we had arrived ahead of the rations, so had to eat what the Germans had left behind – hard biscuits and jam.

We worked long hours but there was always a lot to do in our free time. As there were many RAF and Army units near and Ghent was a leave centre, we were inundated with invitations to parties and privileged to have good ENSA shows, Sadler's Wells ballet, West End shows, the Belgian National Orchestra, all taking place in the Garrison Theatre, the Royal Opera House.

---

[2] Named after Dr Fritz Todt, a German Civil Engineer employed by Hitler to organise forced labour and to take charge of building the West Wall fortifications.

Our first Christmas in Belgium was bitterly cold and we had little heating. Frost formed on our hair as we marched to the office in the mornings. Some girls wore their sea-boot stockings in bed. Our Christmas lunch came out of a tin, but was very good. We had a dance in the local casino to thank the people of Ghent for their hospitality and a Christmas party for the children, when we distributed clothes sent over for them from UK.

Then came New Year's Day 1945 and the breakthrough in the Ardennes by the Germans... all RAF airfields on the continent were attacked. The Polish squadron based on the airfield behind our HQ was out on patrol, which was fortunate, because the Luftwaffe shot up all the aircraft on the ground. The flags of welcome to the British in the streets of Ghent were quickly taken indoors.

This setback didn't last long. As more WAAF were posted in we moved into St Peter's convent, previously used by German servicewomen. It was still occupied by nuns and we bought eggs from them for 10d each, a great luxury for us. By now I had been promoted to sergeant and Mentioned in Dispatches. The convent was some distance from HQ so transport was provided, but if missed, or not available, we travelled by tram. I drove one of these on VE Day, the driver insisting, and there was much clanging of bells. At the tram terminus we used to see relatives waiting outside, hoping to be reunited with loved ones released from Belsen and we saw some of these returning ... a very sorry sight.

85 Group WAAF took part in a VE Day parade and the most impressive of all, the Farewell to Brussels parade in the Parc du Cinquantenaire. All WAAF and RAF were represented and there was a fly-past of aircraft.

Later in November 1945 we moved to Hamburg, travelling by train, wrapped in blankets, it was very cold. We stopped in the middle of the night for a meal in, I think, the railway sidings at

Dusseldorf. The WAAF sergeants were billeted outside the perimeter of the camp in a maisonette, and often in the early days when we set off for duty in the morning, we would see swastikas scratched out in the dirt of the path. It didn't worry us.

By Spring 1946 people were being demobbed, and I was demobbed in March, travelling by sea from Cuxhaven to Hull enroute to Wythall for clearance. I think I slept in seven different beds in seven nights on this journey.

I think I was very lucky to have been a WAAF and to have served with HQ No. 85 Group.

85 Group WAAFs in the orchard at Bon Acceuil, 1944

# An Ode to the Yanks

*Poem from the autograph book of the late Betty Ward*

Thanks for the memory
Of chewing gum and spam,
The processed eggs and ham,
And tho' the rhyme is rotten
We are grateful to a man,
Oh thank you so much.

Thanks for the memory
Of crazy guys in jeeps,
Of friends we've made for keeps,
And of their varied accents
That gave us all the creeps
Oh, thank you so much.

Many's the time we have sniggered
At each others fancy notions
We all had the same devotions
Fighting wasn't fun, but Boy! we won.

So thanks for the memory
Of Roosevelt's Lease and Lend
And Boys, you can depend
Our gratitude for helping us
Will never never end.
Oh thank you so much.

# 5. *Tributes to the WAAF*

In the spate of books published after the war, there was very little, if any, mention of the WAAF who served, and some girls wondered if we had ever been in the RAF at all, or if we had been invisible. But however late it came, thanks for our help did eventually arrive, and as we all like to be thanked for good work done, I reproduce two letters received from ex-RAF men. The first is from David Carmichael of Canada which was published in Air Mail, Oct-Dec 2000.

*For 50 years I have put off writing to offer my recognition to the WAAF groundcrew who displayed such attention to their duties during the war. I was a flying instructor at RAF Upavon.*

*During the summer months the WAAF ground duty was comfortable but, during the winter months when temperatures fell, their duties were more difficult and dangerous too.*

*When we pilots arrived for our morning take offs the windscreens would be scraped of frost and ready for us. The girls would have to crawl along the cold wing, open a panel, crank the engine using a hand crank and remain there until the engine started or, if this failed, begin all over again. Once the engine started, they in the slipstream of the propeller would remove the crank and secure the panel before sliding back along the cold wing and back off the wing to the ground. Once run up was complete they would crawl under the wing to remove the chocks. Their tasks complete, a thumbs up would be given before they walked back to their flight shack for warmth.*

*God, how I admired their efforts! And, of course, they were there when we had finished flying to shut the aircraft down. They were always cheery with a "Good morning" in the mornings and a "Cheerio" at night.*

*Many times, in reviewing parts of my life, I have thought of those girls and how rough some of their duties were. I now feel fulfilled in my duties by submitting a belated but sincere "Thank you Ladies."*

**David Carmichael**

---

A second letter came from the President of the Air Gunners Association.

---

*Thanks yet again to a member of the WAAF Association. Our WAAF at Elvington[3] is now the possessor of a pair of regulation stockings. She is now proudly serving with the Air Gunners in the Gunnery Leader's office.*

*On behalf of the Air Gunners' Association I would once again like to say how much we appreciate your kind help and that of your members and I hope our model will be a constant reminder to those who visit the museum of the vital part these young ladies played in their service with the RAF.*

*It is unfair to select any one category but I must personally say how much I appreciated the MT drivers on my squadrons. In the most appalling weather conditions they would take us out to our aircraft, wishing us luck and offering encouragement. On our return at all hours of the night, no matter how cold and miserable they must so often have been, there was always a smile and a warm welcome for us. They were the last contact we had before take-off and the first on our return. They always held a special place in our hearts and they still do.*

**Norman Storey**

---

[3] The Air Gunners have a memorial at the Yorkshire Air Museum, Elvington which has a mannequin in WAAF uniform as one of the exhibits.

These 3 MT drivers. L-R are Florence Mahoney, Marie Topp and Betty Rook, at RAF Worth Matravers, July 1944.]

MT Driver (name unknown), at Shenley Park Hostel, with Hillman car. RAF Bletchley Park, 1942.

The MT Drivers were employed to drive many different vehicles, from the staff cars – a more glamorous duty, with a VIP sitting in the back, or the Station Commander, with his standard flying from the bonnet, down to the ubiquitous Hillman, or the lorries used to distribute coal or collect laundry bundles, or to ferry aircrews out to their aircraft and collect them after their operations, some to drive ambulances or the unwieldy-looking Queen Mary transporters. Other duties were to drive the fuel bowsers or ammunition trailers out to the waiting aircraft (see below).

*I had the pleasure of working with F/Mech ladies and can personally vouch for their technical skills and gutsy endurance of gashed fingers, chilblains and shocking colds, while working out on frozen, windswept runways. Many a tear was shed quietly in some corner, scorning male sympathy, and many a leg-pull was made by the men but returned by the girls with interest. Their smiles and constant efforts to look good under the grease and oil certainly boosted the morale of the airmen.*

**Mr P.G.R. Duff**

# Ladies in Blue

*Author unknown*

You who were the ladies in blue
May the living God bless you
Though world-wise matron or mature kid
Accept our thanks for all you did
Our meals were served, our 'chutes were packed
And you provided what we lacked
For, be very well aware
Your greatest service, was just being there.

---

The above verse, sent recently to one of our ladies, was apparently written by a one-time crew member of a Lancaster bomber about the WAAFs on his station.

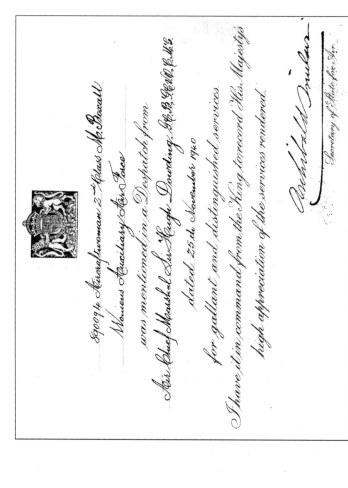

Just one example of the many awards airwomen received for their dedication to their duties, and kept by them with their other treasured mementoes.

# 6. *Awards to WAAF Personnel*

Awards for gallantry were given to WAAF, and these included two George Crosses and six Military Medals. In a letter, Leo Marks, the SOE[4] code-breaker, told me that over a dozen WAAF were among his best code-breakers. Some WAAF, after Wireless operating or other training in the Air Force, were transferred (often at their own request) into the FANY's[5] and after more vigorous training, landed either by parachute or a small, coastal vessel on the continent. They acted as couriers or wireless operators with the Maquis[6] or organised new groups to harass the enemy behind their lines. (The Wireless operators sent information back to Britain, their equipment carried in a suitcase, and always on the move to avoid being caught by the enemy) Their courage was outstanding. Some were captured, tortured and executed.

Girls on duty carried on with vital work during bombardment from enemy aircraft, staying at their posts even as buildings disintegrated around them.

Military OBEs and MBEs, and over two and a half thousand Mentions in Despatches were awarded to others for their dedicated service.

---

[4] SOE. Special Operations Executive- Coders.

[5] FANY. First Aid Nursing Yeomanry - Founded in World War 1, and still operating today.

[6] Maquis. French guerrilla bands, working behind the lines to damage German communications.

WAAF German linguists were promoted to Sergeant, and posted to the East Coast of England, where they kept a listening watch on German aircraft radio frequencies, even themselves giving instructions to the pilots to divert them from their bombing course. These girls did not enlighten their families about their work. They were obliged to sign official secrecy documents, which some still feel bound by.

This year, (2004), a national memorial to honour ALL women, whether service or civilian who served this country through the war, will be built in Whitehall, London. Due to the dedication and single-mindedness of some ATS ex-members, with backing from some members of the Government and thousands of letters and support from this country and overseas, their battle to have this memorial erected has been won.

Through the years there have been oral and written acknowledgment of the work done by women in all walks of life, memorials have been mounted in churches around the country, but this will be the first time a National memorial will be erected to ALL women, Air Raid Wardens, Land Army, Munition workers, the WVS and canteen workers, the Red Cross, and we do not forget the ladies who took into their homes, refugees and children evacuated from cities and cared for them. Neither do we forget the mothers who cared for younger children and kept the home fires burning until the fathers returned from combat, coping with food rationing and shortages.

This long-awaited memorial will also serve as a tangible centre to commemorate those who did not survive the conflict.

---

This book is intended to show the kind of life lived and the work carried out by airwomen, many hardly out of their teens, who spent years in the service of Britain, and I leave the last words to Dorothy Daniel and Pat Tasker.

# I Remember...

*Dorothy Daniel née Hefford*

I remember in '42 I joined the WAAF, a girl in blue.
2029808, hurry on parade and don't be late.
Shoulders straight, heads held high,
Swinging arms towards the sky.
I'll never forget as we marched along
In the wind and rain on Morecambe prom.
Girls from all over the British Isles
When I think of us all I have to smile.
Learning to drive I thought was for me,
So I passed my test and joined the MT.
Lorries and cars and driving at night.
Roads all blacked out and so little light,
Keep with the convoy, don't lose your way,
With my heart in my mouth I longed for the day.
In the icy grip of winter's dawn,
pyjamas under Battledress to try and keep warm.
Round to the dispersals, dropping off the crew,
Say a little inward prayer, come back safely do.
Queueing at the cookhouse with your spoon, knife and fork,
Or meeting at the NAAFI for a friendly little talk.
There were glad days, sad days, laughter, some tears,
But the comradeship and togetherness
I remember through the years.
I still recall that old refrain
When we sang together "We'll meet again".
Where are you now, I wish I knew
My friends of the past in Air Force blue?

# Dear 2029808

*Pat Tasker née Stocking*

Dear 2029808, I had to write I couldn't wait,
I well remember those days in blue
When all our lives were fresh and new,
When hearts were proud-tho' sometimes sad
And the things we did were often mad.
Watching the dawn come up over the "Flights"
When the lads had been out for one of their "nights"
Counting them in with bated breath
Praying they all had cheated death.
The trip to the cookhouse in early morning
(Just in time for an air-raid warning)
Smelling of petrol and not perfume
Still-the admin types gave us plenty of room!
Yes. The friends that we made in those far off days
Helped us get through the war in our different ways
Making beds for each other when coming in late
Explaining ourselves at the Guardroom Gate.
The boiling troughs for the cutlery wash
No one could call that idea very "posh".
Parading here and marching there and
The sudden posting to heaven knew where
But in a way I'm glad to have been
A part of that glorious, frightening scene
When thousands of people we never knew
Were also girls in Air Force blue.
It's good to live in a land that's free,
Says 2148053.

# *More books of interest from Woodfield*

## A Waaf at War by Diana Lindo

This book has proved extremely popular. It tells the story of a WAAF MT driver, who clocked up thousands of miles in her trusty Hillman Staff Car during the years 1941-46. She travelled all over wartime Britain in the course of her duties and her many experiences are sure to rekindle memories for those who also served in the WAAF during the wartime years.

**softback | 120pages | £7.95**

## Lambs in Blue by Rebecca Barnett

When 19-year-old Rebecca Barnett and her friends left their office jobs on Tyneside in 1941 to join the armed forces and do their bit for the war effort, they little imagined that they would end up in a tropical island paradise. But that's exactly what happened when they were posted to Koggala, Ceylon as WAAF teleprinter operators. There they found a hot-house climate, beautiful beaches, palm trees, fabulous sunsets and 2,500 servicemen... Adventure and romance were sure to follow – and indeed they did! Rebecca recounts the adventures of herself and her friends in an entertaining and easy-going style in this warmly nostalgic and good-humoured memoir of one Waaf's very unusual war.

**softback | 196 pages | £9.95**

## Tales of a Bomber Command Waaf by Sylvia Pickering

This book is composed almost exclusively of correspondence which Sylvia either sent to or received from friends and family during the wartime years. We must be grateful for her secretarial training which prompted her to keep all this material, which now provides a fascinating and historically valuable insight into the everyday lives of the young men and women of the wartime RAF.

Sylvia's story takes place in the 'bomber county' of Lincolnshire and we follow her on active duty to the Armoury Sections at RAF Cottesmore and RAF Coningsby.

In her letters, the voice of Sylvia's youthful self describes such diverse off-duty pursuits as learning to dance the tango, visits to the cinema, the potency of pink gin, the problems of transport in the blackout, and many other wartime irritations.

Also prominently featured are the joys and heartbreaks of Sylvia's inevitable romantic entanglements; in particular her relationship with 'Roo' – a young Australian airman with whom she lost touch (as was so often the case in those days) when he was 'posted elsewhere'. It was to be 50 years before she discovered what had happened to him...

**softback | 196 pages | £9.95**

## More Tales of a Bomber Command Waaf by Sylvia Pickering

This second book about Sylvia's life as a WAAF is also composed mostly of correspondence from the wartime years. In it she is posted from RAF Coningsby as a "disturbing influence" and a "subversive element" only to prove her detractors wrong in a most satisfactory way when posted to H.Q. 5 Group (Bomber Command) at Moreton Hall.

We meet two Australians – Ken, a mid-upper gunner of 460 RAAF Squadron and Tom, a rear gunner of 463 RAAF Squadron. Their rivalry for Sylvia's affections is charted in Ken's playful and hopeful letters and there is a wonderful tale of an evening out with Tom spent getting drunk just to find our what others "found so enjoyable" about the process. Tom became a POW in Stalag Luft 7 after being shot down by night fighters and his report on the conditions on their forced march and the map of the route are dreadful reminders of the privations faced by those who shared this experience.

It is wonderful to be able to read the letters from Jimmy, Sylvia's fiancé; remarkable, eloquent love letters of the sort which feature less and less in modern relationships.

Peace saw Sylvia finally able to indulge her passion for horses, find happiness in her marriage and, at the age of eighty, write her second remarkable book...

**softback | 264 pages | £9.95**

## Radar Days by Gwen Arnold

Radar Days is a book notable for its humour and charm, as well as being a historically interesting record of activities at one of the top-secret radar bases that guarded British shores during world War Two. Gwen Arnold takes her readers on an entertaining journey from her formative years in the seaside town of Bournemouth to her wartime role at Bawdsey Manor RDF Station near Felixtowe in Suffolk, where she was stationed for most of the war. On the way there are humorous and well-observed vignettes of her family life, her first experiences of employment in her home town, her early romantic liaisons and her induction into the armed forces... all of which combine into an affectionate picture of what it was like to grow up in the 1930s and to serve in the wartime Women's Auxiliary Air Force.

**softback | 180 pages | £9.95**

## Searching in the Dark by Peggy Butler

Peggy has unearthed her wartime diary/scrap book along with many photos and snippets of information and created a book that will bring back many memories for those who served in the RAF in World War 2.

All the text was written when Peggy was just 20 years old and serving at RAF bases in Tannach, Scotland and Bawdsey Manor, Suffolk and she has wisely resisted the temptation to re-edit it, allowing instead the voice of her younger self to reveal her thoughts and feelings as they were at the time – the result is very entertaining.

**softback | 200 pages | £7.95**

## Why Did We Join? by Eileen Smith

*"Why did we join? Why did we join? Why did we join the Royal Air Force?*
*Ten bob a week. Nothing to eat. Damn great boots making blisters on your feet..."*
These were the words that Eileen Smith and her pals used to sing as they route-marched round the country lanes near Wilmslow whilst on basic training for the WAAF. Eileen answers the song's question herself in this charming and nostalgic book, in which she recalls the many experiences and friendships of her years in uniform. Although facilities were spartan and the work less than glamorous, she and her fellow WAAFs knew that this would be a time of their lives they would never forget.

In early 1944 Eileen (known as 'Smithy' to her service pals) was posted to RAF East Kirkby, an operational bomber station, home to 57 Squadron and 630 Squadron. Allied raids on Germany were at their peak, as were the losses of Bomber Command aircrews. With the young flyers facing the very real possibility of 'getting the chop' on their next mission, romantic liaisons took on an extra dimension and Eileen does well to recapture the emotionally-charged atmosphere, which inevitably led to all manner of relationships ... and all kinds of trouble. There are many laughs to be had at the high jinks she and her fellow servicemen and women indulged in to relive the tensions of their situation, but there is sadness too, of course, for the many young men who did not live to see the end of hostilities... A good balance is struck, however, and the result is an entertaining and a historically valuable record of wartime life in the WAAF.

**softback | 154 pages | £9.95**

## Nina & Vic edited by Janine Harrington

The publication of this book marks the fulfilment of a promise made over 60 years ago in the summer of 1944, when a young RAF officer told his WAAF fiancée that one day he would write the story of their love as an inspiration to all those who read it.

He never had the chance to do so. On the night of 26/27 November 1944, Mosquito DK292 of 192 Squadron in which he was navigator, failed to return from a mission to Munich. His body was never found. Nina was devastated, but determined to put the heartbreak of war behind her and eventually found a new love, was married and raised a family - but for 50 years her unworn wartime wedding dress remained at the back of her wardrobe, along with hundreds of letters, still in their original envelopes, her diaries, a nail from the gate of the church where she and Vic had become engaged, old photographs and a pair of his silk flying gloves - a testimony to the love they shared and lost.

In the early 1990s Nina's daughter Janine began to work with her mother on a book to fulfil Vic's promise. Together they joined the RAF 100 Group Association, based in Norfolk, which enabled them to talk to Vic's former best friend and other colleagues and begin to trace his final, fateful journey. The result is this book, told mostly in Nina and Vic's own words via their letters, but supported by diary entries, telegrams, photographs and other wartime memorabilia - together they tell a fascinating and moving story.

**softback | 368 pages | £15.00**

**Corduroy Days** by Josephine Duggan Rees

This funny and warm-hearted depiction of the life of a 'Land Girl' in World War II has already won praise from readers of all ages.

Josephine Duggan Rees was just 17 years old at the outbreak of World War II, and was one of the thousands of young women who responded to the Government's call for female workers to take up jobs in the countryside by joining the Women's Land Army.

These 'Land Girls' took to farm work with energy and enthusiasm, prepared to tackle any task, long before the days of 'Women's Lib'. It was hard work, but the Spartan working conditions, unreliable tractors, truculent cart-horses and the merciless teasing of male co-workers could not dampen the author's enthusiasm for country life. Buoyed up by the camaraderie of her fellow Land Girls and her love of the countryside, she battled against adversity, finding romance amongst the haystacks and finally setting off with a new husband for a lifetime involved with farming and rural pursuits.

Former Land Girls, in particular, will be reminded of their own youthful experiences, but there is much to be enjoyed by any reader of this charming evocation of youthful experiences in those far-off 'Corduroy Days'.

**softback | 228 pages | £9.95**

Woodfield have also published two more books by Josephine Duggan Rees:

**Boys & Other Animals** is her charming depiction of her chaotic life as a farmer's wife and mother to a family of four boys in rural Sussex in the 1950s, 60s and 70s.

A **Portrait of Slindon** is her coulourful history of this peaceful South Downs village.

All the above books may be purchased by mail order direct from the publishers by writing to: Dept AWW, Woodfield Publishing, Bognor Regis, West Sussex PO21 5EL

**Tel** 01243 821234 ~ **e-mail** orders@woodfieldpublishing.com

For further details of all our books visit our website at

# www.woodfieldpublishing.com

we have many more titles about the RAF, World War 2 and other subjects.

**Do you have an interesting story to tell?** We are always interested in hearing from new authors. Please contact us at the above address / phone number.